Bill Gates

Businessman and Co-founder of Tech Giant Microsoft

(The Truth About Bill Gates's Life and Business Success Revealed)

Sheila Corbett

Published By **Phil Dawson**

Sheila Corbett

Bill Gates: Businessman and Co-founder of Tech Giant Microsoft (The Truth About Bill Gates's Life and Business Success Revealed)

ISBN   978-1-77485-763-2

Legal & Disclaimer

The information contained in this ebook is not designed to replace or take the place of any form of medicine or professional medical advice. The information in this ebook has been provided for educational & entertainment purposes only.

The information contained in this book has been compiled from sources deemed reliable, and it is accurate to the best of the Author's knowledge; however, the Author cannot guarantee its accuracy and validity and cannot be held liable for any errors or omissions. Changes are periodically made to this book. You must consult your doctor or get professional medical advice before using any of the suggested remedies, techniques, or information in this book.

Upon using the information contained in this book, you agree to hold harmless the Author from and against any damages, costs, and expenses, including any legal fees potentially resulting from the application of any of the

TABLE OF CONTENTS

Introduction 1

Chapter 1: The Early Life...................5

Chapter 2: The Personal Life...........11

Chapter 3: Microsoft Basics: Microsoft Basic 19

Chapter 4: Prosecution Of Antitrust-Related Violation 29

Chapter 5: Investments And Ventures 35

Chapter 6: Energy And The Environment...................................39

Chapter 7: Charity 43

Chapter 8: Works Of Literature 52

Chapter 9: A View Of Bill Gates And Microsoft 61

Chapter 10: Bill Gates & Paul Allen - Secrets Of Legendary Business Partnerships Through The Eyes Of Numerology...................................101

Chapter 11: Bill Gates Inventions-
Top-Greatest Hits And Misses 144

Chapter 12: Education And Marriage
....162

Conclusion 182

Introduction

William Henry Gates III (born on October 28th 1955) is a famous American developer, entrepreneur and financial supporter, developer and Philanthropist. Along with his late beloved colleague Paul Allen, he is a Microsoft Corporation donor. In his time with Microsoft, Gates held the post of director, CEO president Chief Programming Engineer in addition to being the largest shareholder of the company up to May 2014. Gates is widely regarded as an one of the more impressive and renowned business geniuses during the 1970s and the 1980s, when the microcomputer revolution took over. Gates was born in Seattle and lived in Belmont in a suburb that was close to of the city. He and his friend Allen developed the first personal computer they founded Microsoft Inc. The company quickly grew into the biggest business software company around the globe. Gates was the company's chief executive an executive between 1975 and 2000, until he was replaced by his co-founder Steve Ballmer to take over when he was promoted to a position at the top , the CEO. Gates was the manager of the highest management team, and eventually rose to the post of chief program architect. He was scrutinized in the latter part of 1990s due to his commercial practices that were seen as contrary to the seriousness. A number of court rulings have back the conclusion. On June 8, 2008 Gates was promoted to an entry-level job at Microsoft as well as regular duties for the Bill and Melinda Gates Foundation, a private foundation for charitable causes which he and his former wife, Melinda Gates, founded in 2000.

The month of February was when he stepped out as the Microsoft's executive group. At the time, he was hoping to be hired again as an innovation consultant to support Satya Nadella Microsoft's new CEO. Gates quit his position in the board of Microsoft as well as Berkshire Hathaway in March 2020 to concentrate on his charitable initiatives, which include sustainability globally, advancement and wellness and education. Gates has been listed on Forbes's list of most wealthy people since the year 1987. In the years 2010 to 2013 he was not on Forbes' list Gates was a regular holder of his Forbes designation of being the world's wealthiest person from 1995 until 2017.

In October of 2017 the two were beaten in the race by Jeff Bezos, the founder and CEO of Amazon with an estimated total asset value at $90.6 billion, as compared with Gates' $89.9 billion. Gates is estimated to have an assets worth $144 billion at the time of his May 2021 election which would make the fourth most wealthy person. After leaving Microsoft's day-today operations at the end of 2008 Gates is involved in a number of charitable and commercial projects. Gates founded and serves as the CEO of various businesses that include BEN, Cascade Investment, bgC3 and TerraPower.

By way of through the Bill and Melinda Gates Foundation which is widely regarded as the largest private charity in the world and has given significant amounts of cash to a variety of charitable organizations as well as logical examination programs. He led a mid-twentieth-century immunization campaign via the institution, which contributed significantly to the eradication of the wild poliovirus in Africa. Gates along with Warren Buffett formed The Giving Pledge in 2010 where they, along with others billionaires pledged to donate the equivalent of half their fortune to charitable causes.

Chapter 1: The Early Life

Bill Gates was born on October 28, 1955 in Seattle, Washington. William H. Gates Sr. was born (1925-2020) as well as Mary Maxwell Gates (1929-1994) are his parents. His ancestors are from English, German, and Scottish/Irish origin.

His father was an acclaimed attorney and his mother was employed with First Interstate BancSystem and the United Way of America as an executive. Gates his paternal grandfather, J. W. Maxwell was a president of a public bank and Gates Great-Grandfather's maternal grandfather was also a bank president. Gates is the mother of two daughters: Kristi (Kristianne), who is older Kristi (Kristianne), who is older, and Libby and Libby, who are younger.

In spite of the fact he's the fourth member of his family, he's identified by the name of William Gates III, or "Three Pointer" (i.e. three) due to the fact that the surname of his father ends with "II." When Gates was just seven year old, the family lived in a home in Seattle's Sand Point neighborhood that was destroyed by a twister that was rare. Gates was aware early on in his existence that his family's needs forced him to enter an attorney's career. His family was an avid member of the Congregational Christian Churches, a Protestant Reformed denomination, when as a kid. Gates was an unusually young man in his twenties, and he was a victim of bullying in his youth.

One of the attendees told me, "It didn't matter if it was pickleball, hearts or going to the pier for swimming; there was always an award for winners and there was always the punishment for losing." He attended an private Lakeside preparatory school around 13 and developed his first computer-based program. The mother's club of Lakeside School used the proceeds from the scavenge sale to purchase an Teletype Model 33 ASR terminal as well as a piece in PC-related time the General Electric (GE) PC for students while they were in the eighth grade.

Gates discovered a passion for programming using the GE framework using BASIC He was exempted from math class in pursuit of his dream. With this platform Gates developed his first software for PC that was a basic game which let players play with the computer. The computer piqued Gates' attention due to its capability to execute programming instructions perfectly each time. When it was decided that the Mothers Club contribution had been used up, Gates and his associates considered other alternatives, including DEC Minicomputers PDP. One of these frameworks was PDP-10 that had an agreement to the Computer Center Corporation (CCC) that prohibited Gates, Paul Allen, Ric Weiland as well as Gates close friend and former colleague, Kent Evans, from making use of bugs in the framework to get free PC time during the middle of the year.

To raise funds to fund their activities, the four co-workers came together to form to raise money, the four counterparts formed Lakeside Programmers Club. They offered to discover the flaws in CCC's product, as a reward for longer time on their PCs following the termination in the boycott. Instead of employing the framework remotely using Teletype, Gates may have visited CCC's offices and looked at source code for other projects using the framework, like Fortran, Lisp, and machine language. The CCC strategy was implemented until the year 1970 after which the CCC was dissolved of existence.

The following year an Lakeside teacher asked Gates as well as Evans to help with the computerization of the school's scheduling system for classes which gave them access to PCs and autonomy in the process. They put in many hours of effort to make the program functional in time for senior school. In the midst of this, Gates went to Allen to assist him in the process of completing the building for Lakeside.

At the age of 17 Gates and Allen established Traf-O Data an initiative to make traffic counters reliant on their Intel 8008 CPU. He was a student at Harvard University where he was an active member of both the ROTC as well as the Kirkland House. In 1972, he was working as a page for the congressional within the House of Representatives and after graduation, he was awarded numerous distinctions, including being a National Merit Scholar, accepted to the Phi Beta Kappa Society, and awarded the Gates

Cambridge Scholarship, named the most likely to succeed, and also won the NCAA High Jump Championship Award. He continued to study at Harvard following graduation before joining Microsoft. Gates left Harvard in the year following however Ballmer continued and was awarded the prestigious Magnacum laude. Ballmer became the successor to Gates as Microsoft's Chief Executive for a lengthy time and he was in the position until 2014, when he left the position. In reaction to one of several puzzles that were posed during the course on combinatorics by a teacher Harry Lewis, Gates devised the flapjack arrangement algorithm.

For over 30 years, his answer was the world record for the most speedy form that is only 2% more efficient. Together along with Harvard PC researcher Christos Papadimitriou He codified and distributed his solution. Through the spring of 1974 Gates continued to communicate with Paul Allen and accompanied him to Honeywell. The MITS Altair 8800, based on the Intel 8080 CPU, was launched the year 1975 Gates and Allen recognized the opportunity to launch their own software business. While Bill Gates had received a award to pursue his education at Harvard but the decision was made to take a year off and launch Microsoft in the year 1975. The Gates family was supportive of his decision after they realized the seriousness Bill was about setting up his own business. "If the situation didn't go as planned I would have the option of going back to Harvard," he said of his decision to drop out of Harvard. I was on sabbatical for the duration of my sabbatical.

Chapter 2: The Personal Life

Gates is an avid reader of all types of books. The walls of his home library are adorned with quotes from philosophy and literature and include F. Scott Fitzgerald's words that are engraved into the ceiling of his classic book, The Great Gatsby. He also loves scaffolding tennis, golfing, and scaffolding. His schedule is set by him on a minute-by minute basis, much like the president of the United States' schedule. In spite of his riches and multiple traveling, Gates travelled on business aircrafts in regular economy class (economy level) up to 1997 when he bought an aircraft for his own. He purchased the plane in 1994. Gates made a deal to purchase the Codex Leicester, a collection of logical work by Leonardo da Vinci, for US $30.8 million.

He was alleged to have bought $30m in the year 1998 his first marine painting of 1885, Lost on the Grand Banks It was the highest price ever paid for an American painting at the time. He found out he was blind in the year 2016.

Separation and Matrimony

On January 1, 1994 Bill Gates married Melinda French on Lanai Island, Hawaii. Melinda began her career at Microsoft in 1987 and they first met in 1987. The day before their weddingday, Melinda offered Gates permission to give a little of his energy towards his former wife, the financial manager Ann Winblad, on the day of their wedding. Jennifer, Rory, and Phoebe, Bill and Melinda's three children. in Medina, Washington, the family lives in a mansion that has been shielded by earth on the hill that overlooks Lake Washington. The local charges for the house included US $1.06 million for 2009 based upon an assessed value total in the amount of US $147.5 millions.

The 60-foot (18-meter) pool, with submerged music structures along with an 2,500-square-foot (230-square-meter) entertainment center as well as an area of 1,000 square feet (93-square-meter) dining space are among the highlights of the home's 66,000-square-foot (6,100-square-meter) home. Bill Gates and Melinda Gates declared their arrangement to split after their marriage for 27 years, in 2021. 34 years of being together. Although they had previously pledged to remain married until the end of time They both said that they were completely happy for each other and are looking forward to the next stage of their lives as singles.

A long-time friend who is now fighting accusations of legality that may damage an individual's image, has tried to disclose information that links Bill Gates to Jeffrey Epstein that is believed to have triggered their divorce. But, according to Mrs. Gates, who spoke to The Wall Street Journal, this was just one of the many reasons behind their divorce. In the month of August 2021, their well-publicized divorce was officially approved.

Jeffrey Epstein's relationship according to an New York Times report, Gates's relationship with sex offender accused Jeffrey Epstein began in 2011 only a few months following the conviction of Epstein. The relationship continued for a number of years and included Melinda remembering a trip to Epstein's home during the autumn of 2013 even though she was clearly uncomfortable.

Gates declared in 2011 that the lifestyle of Epstein was completely unique and sort of attractive despite his conviction that it did not be suitable for the accused.

The extent of the relationship among Gates and Epstein isn't clear. The majority of the time, Gates talked about his relationship and friendship with Epstein: "I had the pleasure of having him meet me. I had no personal or business ties to Epstein." In spite of Epstein's reputation, Gates visited him "on regularly." On board 2013 Gates had at least one trip on Epstein's notorious. As per the reports, Epstein along with Gates talked about his Gates Foundation and the generosity of. In a 2019 meeting However, Gates absolutely denied the connection with Epstein as well as his Gates Foundation, as well as his charitable foundation in general.

Gates declared at the end of August in 2021 that he had meetings with Epstein as he believed that Epstein could donate money to charities, yet nothing was born from the concept. Gates also said that investing in his energy and offering him the chance of being in the room was a huge mistake.

Public Image

The perception regarding Bill Gates has shifted over the course of. In the beginning, he was perceived as a ruthless, but magnificent burglar an aristocrat, a geek turned into a tycoon. Since the creation of the Bill and Melinda Gates Foundation in 2000, and especially after his departure as the CEO of Microsoft and focusing his efforts on charitable causes which has amounted to greater than 50 billion dollars on matters like poverty, health, and education. From the dominant technocrat to the noble friend in need a huggable , extremely rich person , and a techno-altruist, he was featured on magazines' covers and questioned for his views on the most important topics like global welfare and environmental changes.

Yet, a alteration in his general perception came in 2021, when he declared that He and Melinda were breaking up. The inclusion of this continued relationship brought out facts, heartfelt pleas for women who worked for him, an extended extra-conjugal matter as well as a relationship with the sentenced youngster sex dealer

Jeffrey Epstein. This resulted in a major loss of the public perception of Gates. On June 20, 2021 The New Republic depicted Gates as an oligarch as well as just one more terrifying wealthy person.

Religion

Gates highlighted his belief in an interview in Rolling Stone, saying, "The religious values that are ethically rooted I believe that they are extremely fundamental." Our children were raised in a highly religious atmosphere They attended Melinda's Catholic Church, which I currently go to. I've been blessed and am obligated to the rest of the world to work to make things more palatable. Also, it's an unshakeable conviction. In another way it's like having moral conviction. In a similar gathering in 2014 where he said that he was in agreement with scientists such as Richard Dawkins that humans feel the need to believe in mythology of creation.

We looked for false explanations for these phenomena before we started to experience illness, the climate , and other similar things. Science has now taken over an area which religion was once a part of but not the entire. The mystery of the world and its excellence however are generally awe-inspiring and there is no reason to explain why they are the way they have become. The idea that it was created through an assortment of unnatural numbers appears an unkind comment, which is why it's laughed at. I am adamant that putting your trust in God is a good idea however, I'm not aware of the decisions you take in your life due to it.

Political Engagement

Political and business guidelines for products. In a speech in front of the United States Senate in 1998, Gates criticized the need for the establishment of business norms that are specific to product. Gates declared that a sustained rejection of Trump "would be an embarrassment" and amounts to "dramatic actions" in the 18th of February, 2021 following the fact that Facebook and Twitter removed Donald Trump from their platforms in connection with elections in 2020. United States presidential elections, which led to an 2021 United States Capitol assault. Gates warned that the division of people with different political views in a multitude of informal groups could result in the polarization of society.

"I am not convinced that preventing anyone who had a respectable amount of votes in the presidential election well but not a larger percentage for the rest time would sound fantastic." Antibody certificates for COVID-19 in the outbreak in April 2021. Gates was ridiculed for proposing that pharmaceutical companies obtain COVID-19 vaccination certificates. The inquiry was motivated because of the fear that it could stop other nations that aren't fortunate from getting sufficient antibodies.

"Gates speaks as if each life loss in India is inexplicable however, eventually the West will come in," Tara Van Ho from the University of Essex said, "when actually both the US and UK have their backs on the shoulders of those who are creating states by refusing to sever IP rights insurance." "It's revolting."

Chapter 3: Microsoft Basics: Microsoft

Basic

After looking at an Altair 8800 within the Jan. 1975 issue of Popular Electronics, Gates contacted Micro Instrumentation and Telemetry Systems (MITS) to inform them that he and his colleagues were developing the development of a BASIC translation for this platform. Yes, Gates and Allen were not equipped with an Altair and had not yet create code for it; all they had to do was evaluate the advantages of MITS. MITS the president Ed Roberts agreed to meet with them to present an exhibit during the time of a month they came up with an Altair emulator to be used as a minicomputer, and an BASIC translator.

The event was held inside MITS's headquarter at Albuquerque, New Mexico; it was a huge success, which resulted in a contract with MITS to provide the mediation in Altair BASIC. Allen was employed by MITS and, on November 25, 1975 Gates disappeared from Harvard to join Allen at MITS. Their first office was located in

Albuquerque and Allen called their company "Miniature Soft,"" an amalgamation that referred to "microcomputer" in addition to "programming." Ric Weiland who was a high school acquaintance of Gates Allen who was their primary representative they sought out.

Within one year, they removed the dash and registered the trademark of the company "Microsoft" to the secretary of state of New Mexico on November 26 in 1976. While Microsoft's Altair BASIC was well-known among PC experts, Gates discovered that a early version had leaked and was widely reproduced and distributed.

In February 1976, he wrote the Open Letter to Hobbyists in the MITS pamphlet in which he stated that more than 90% of users from Microsoft Altair BASIC were no money to pay Microsoft for it , and it was his opinion that Microsoft's Altair "diversion market" was in danger of removing the motivational power of any skilled engineer to provide, transmit the message, and stay up to date with high-quality software. The letter was not liked by a variety of PC experts, however Gates stood firm in his belief that designers of products should be able to ask for installments. In the latter half of 1976 Microsoft began to be independent from MITS. The company continued to create programming languages and systems, which were the beginning steps towards object-oriented programming. On January 1, 1979, the company was relocated out of Albuquerque in New Mexico to Bellevue, Washington. The company's initial five years Gates said he checked and changed the lines of code. He rose through his ranks within the company before becoming the director and later an executive. Donkey Bas is a 1981 PC game that was released with the first version of the PC DOS operating system, that was released alongside the original IBM PC. It's a driving game where the player has to avoid collisions with Jackasses. Gates as well as Neil Konzen collaborated on the game's design.

IBM affiliation

IBM is the primary source of PC products for companies at the time was pushed towards Microsoft in July 1980 over programming for the upcoming PC called which was the IBM PC, after Bill Gates' mother, Mary Maxwell Gates, made reference towards Microsoft as John Opel, IBM's CEO. IBM initially suggested that Microsoft develop its own BASIC interpreter. IBM's delegate also stated they needed a functional framework that could be used for programming, and Gates suggested they contact Digital Research (DRI), the company behind the well-known CP/M operating system. But IBM's talks of Digital Research were insufficient, and they were not able to reach an agreement. In a subsequent meeting with Gates, IBM delegate Jack Sams was able to mention issues with authorization when asked whether Microsoft could develop a feasible framework. In the following months, Gates and Allen advocated using 86-DOSas a viable base like CP/M created in the hands of Tim Paterson of Seattle Computer Products (SCP) for computers. Microsoft entered into a partnership with SCP to be the 86 DOS select authorized specialist , and later the sole owner. In exchange for a one-time payment that was $50,000 Microsoft employed Paterson to alter the operating system on PC and then delivered this the operating system to IBM in the form of PC DOS.

The actual arrangement was a sham that only cost Microsoft just a little money. The distinction made to Microsoft with IBM's approval of their working framework could begin the transition from a private enterprise to the world's top firm in programming. Given his belief that other PC makers would duplicate IBM's PC hardware Gates did not propose transfer of the copyright over the framework's work to IBM. They were able to make the IBM-compatible PC that operated under DOS as a standard. Since Microsoft started talks to negotiate with IBM, Microsoft has become a major player on the market.

The press celebrated Microsoft as being a particularly powerful program for it's IBM PC right away. Gates was asked to confirm if it was "the one who made Microsoft's computer" in PC Magazine. On June 25 1981 Gates was in charge of Microsoft's restructuring that reestablished the company in Washington and named Gates as the president and board administrator along with Paul Allen as vice president. Following the diagnosis of Hodgkin's disease, Allen departed the company at the mid-point of 1983, thus ending the relations with Gates and Allen who was strained for several years due to a conflict over Microsoft shares.

The following year, Gates and Allen patched each other up, and they gave millions of dollars in their school of choice, Lakeside. They remained close until Allen's passing.

Windows

On the 20th of November, 1985 Microsoft along with Gates unveiled the initial version for retail of Microsoft Windows to challenge Apple's Macintosh GUI, which had attracted buyers by its simplicity of use.

In 1988, following making public the announcement about their partnership with IBM to create OS/2, Microsoft released a mostly business-oriented version of Windows officially titled Windows 2.0 that was based on the MS-DOS framework which was previously used and was already preinstalled and bundled along with Word for Windows -- the precursor to Office which we use today as it. Despite the initial success and widespread use in the period there were a variety of issues that arose between the two companies partly to divergent philosophies about the direction to take OS/2's evolution as a design, and the best way to ensure future compatibleness with existing Microsoft products. For over 10 years, the OS/2 framework surpassed DOS in a natural manner until it was time that the DOS display of text was moved to the storage space in conjunction with Windows 95.

Windows XP, followed and is believed to have been the first operating system that is not founded on DOS. Windows 8.1 was the last release of Windows 8.1, the version that was, released prior to Bill Gates handed over the control of the business over to John W. Thompson on February 5 in 2014. The latest version, which was released in 2017 is dubbed Windows 10 and then again Windows 11 in 2021. It was the first time that Microsoft made available one operating system that could be used on tablets, smartphones, as well as desktop computers. All manageable devices are owned by a specific person or company. The first edition of Windows 10 included an interface like its predecessors, however it also had numerous new features, including enhanced security options, including devices encryption; and new or upgraded versions of technologies like Microsoft's Edge Web browser, and the Cortana digital assistant Integration with Microsoft's voice-controlled personal assistant Cortana and a brand new, universal platform for apps to bring together the two distinct apps stores that had two interfaces; and also the ability to increase the size of elements for user interfaces to accommodate various screen sizes with a manner that maintains the clarity of the display.

When fellow colleague Paul Allen was undergoing treatments for cancerous growth in the late 1980s, Gates conspired to reduce Allen's stake in Microsoft by granting him stock options according to Allen. Allen was later to claim in his bio in the 1980s that Gates was "concocting an scheme to fraud me." It was, in essence, the advantage of a soldier." Gates says he has an entirely different recall of the incident. Allen will also refer to Gates notorious tendency to shout during situations. Gates met Microsoft's top executives and program managers regularly and they said they were a bit hostile.

He also lashed out at the group for recognizing flaws in their practices or making suggestions that could harm the long-term interests of the organization. By saying things such as "that is the most ridiculous thing I've encountered" and "why you don't just change your choice by joining in the Peace Corps," he interfered in introductions. The ideals for his revolutionary cause would need to be vigorously defending the case until Gates was completely convinced. He would often say with a laugh, "I'll do it over the weekend," when subordinates seemed to be slow in their steps.

Microsoft employees have complained that Microsoft employees have accused Gates of threatening them. Gates was a programmer during the early days of Microsoft and particularly when it came to changing language components, but his main job for the majority of Microsoft's history was that of director and head. He's not part of the development department since working using Microsoft's TRS-80 Model 100, although the code he wrote was integrated into Microsoft's products until the year 1989. To respond the report of Bill Gates' reporting on Microsoft Excel, Jerry Pournelle declared in 1985:

"Bill Gates is a fan of the program because it's a great hack, not to bring him tons of dollars (although I'm certain it will) and, more importantly, because it's an amazing hack." Gates declared on June 15, 2006 that he would quit Microsoft to dedicate more time to expressing his gratitude. In the process of putting Ray Ozzie in charge of the executive team along with Craig Mundie in charge of long-haul items He gradually split his responsibilities among his two successors. The process took about two years shift all his responsibilities over to Ozzie and Mundie and was completed on the 27th of June in 2008.

Chapter 4: Prosecution Of Antitrust-

Related Violation

Gates supported a variety of rulings that resulted in an antitrust investigation into Microsoft's strategy. Gates provided an affidavit of support of his support for the United States v. Microsoft case in 1998, which only a handful of columnists deemed to be sneaky. Gates as well as analysts David Boies argued about the importance of words like "contend," "concerned," and "we." In the following year when the taped statements were played back in court, the adjudicator could be observed snickering and shaking their head. Even the adjudicator in charge of the case laughed as he made obfuscatory statements and declared "I do not remember" repeatedly during his testimony. Unfortunately, a large number of Gates assertions and denials of ignorance were rebuked by the examiners who used emails that Gates was both a recipient and sender. Gates later explained that he was in opposition to Boies trying to alter his actions and words. "Is you sure that it is true that I was fighting Boies? I acknowledge... the first degree of dishonor towards Boies. "Despite Gates' protests, the authority in charge determined that Microsoft had violated the Sherman Antitrust Act by submitting the syndication, tying and hindering competition.

Post-Microsoft

In the wake of his departure from everyday tasks within Microsoft, Gates has proceeded with awe and humour, while chipping away at different projects.

According to according to the Bloomberg Billionaires Index, Gates was the world's most wealthy person in 2013, when his assets grew to $15.8 billion, to $78.5 billion. At the time of writing most of Gates assets are within Cascade Investment LLC, an company that holds stakes in various companies which include Four Seasons Hotels and Resorts and Corbis Corp. On February 4 of 2014, Gates ventured down as an executive at Microsoft to be a "innovation guide" within the company and was followed by the Chief Executive Officer Satya Nadella.

In a long meeting that was featured within the February 27, 2014 edition of Rolling Stone magazine, Gates presented his views on a variety of topics. At the time of the meeting Gates presented his view on the environment as well as his positive activities in various tech-related organizations, those who work with them, as well as the country of America. Due to an inquiry about the biggest fear he has when he thinks 50 years in the near future Gates said :"... that there are some truly horrible events that could happen in the coming fifty or 100 years however it's unlikely that any of them will be at the level of say 1,000,000 people who you did not expect to die due to a pandemic, or from atomic or bioterrorism. "In an extensive interview, which was published on March 27th, 2014 edition of Rolling Stone magazine, Gates spoke about his views about a wide range of topics.

In the same way, Gates acknowledged development as an "true engine of advancement" and declared that "America's approach to development is better than it ever was." Gates has expressed his concern over the possible harm that brilliance can cause as he posted on Reddit "ask me any question" post, he said: "First, the robots will do a lot of human work and not be super-intelligent. In the past, some considered it beneficial to develop self-driving vehicles and even drones that are available to the public however it could be a while before we'll know if this was a negative thing. Some say flying cars are a dream however, I'm not convinced about the battery longevity of something like that for instance, since we weren't thinking about the many possibilities at the time. However, I think that I'm to Elon Musk and other pioneers who say we should make improvements soon. There's no reason to sit for too long, or to determine how well something works before moving forward with changes , because one day we could regret it!

In a meeting with Baidu's CEO Robin Li, at the TED conference in March 2015 Gates said the company would "highly highly recommend" Nick Bostrom's newest book Super-intelligence: Pathsand Strategies, Dangers during an interview with Gates during the discussion, Gates expressed concern that the world was not adequately prepared for the next epidemic that will hit the streets in the latter part of 2019 with the COVID-19 virus. In March of 2018, Gates met at his home in Seattle with Mohammed bin Salman, the reformist crown sovereign and real ruler in Saudi Arabia, to talk about the possibility of venture opportunities in Saudi Vision 2030. Gates acknowledged in June of 2019, that losing out on the race for portable operating systems against Android was his biggest mistake.

He claimed that the position of being the most dominant was within their reach however, he did criticize the antitrust probe in the time. In the was the same year that Gates got appointed as a member of Bloomberg's New Economy Forum's advisory Board. On March 13 of the 13th of March, 2020 Microsoft made it clear that Bill Gates was stepping down from his positions in Berkshire Hathaway and Microsoft in the hope of committing his time and efforts to noble causes like the environment along with the global economy, health development as well as education. Although he is not a government official or possessing any previous professional training in clinical medicine, Gates has been widely acknowledged as an expert in the COVID-19 outbreak by news outlets.

In any event in 2020, his company established the COVID-19 Therapeutics Accelerator, to accelerate the creation and evaluation of new or repurposed drugs and biologics that treat COVID-19 patients. As in February 2021 Gates declared that Anthony Fauci and he often discuss and collaborate on topics like antibodies and other clinical advancements to combat the disease.

Chapter 5: Investments And Ventures

Gates has a multibillion dollar investment portfolio that includes stakes in many industries. He has also taken part in a variety of ventures that are innovative outside of Microsoft which include: Gates owns a 16 percent stake in AutoNation which is an auto retailer which trades on the New York Stock Exchange (NYSE). Gates created bgC3 LLC an organization for research and a think tank that he created. As of the year 2019, Gates is the largest single investor in Canadian National Railway (CN) which is a Canadian class I railroad for freight. Cascade Investment LLC, a private holding and investment company situated within the United States, was founded and regulated to be controlled by Gates and is located within Kirkland, Washington.

With land holdings of 242,000 square feet of land across 19 states via Cascade Investment, Bill Gates is the most valuable private landowner across the United States. He is the 49th largest property owner within the United States. Gates has helped to finance David Keith's startup, Carbon

Engineering, as an enterprise that generates revenue. Chevron Corporation and Occidental Petroleum are also in support of the venture. The latter is for SCoPEx Keith's study to explore "sun-diminishing" geoengineering that Gates was a major contributor of the money.

Corbis is a digital image permission and rights management corporation established and managed by Gates. The company was previously known as Interactive Home Systems and is now being referred to as Branded Entertainment Network. EarthNow is a Seattle-based company which plans to expand its coverage across the globe using real-time satellite images. Gates is a major financial backer. Eclipse Aviation was a defunct producer for ultralight planes. It was almost immediately that Bill Gates became a key participant in the project. Impossible Foods is a company which develops plant-based alternatives to meat. In 2014-2017 Gates provided a significant portion of his $396 million Patrick O. Brown collected for his company.

Ecolab is a world-wide supplier of sanitation, water, and energy solutions and services for the energy, food medical care, modern and hospitality industries. It was in 2012 that Gates has increased the amount he invested into Ecolab by 10.8 percentage to 25. ResearchGate provides a social media service specifically for academics. Alongside other investors, Gates participated in an investment round of $35 million.

TerraPower is an atomic reactor configuration company created and led by Gates who is working on the most advanced transporting thermal energy facilities for wave reactors to fight climate change.

Breakthrough Energy Ventures is a closed asset for wealthy people seeking a 20-year outlook that "is financing green-friendly companies as well as a vast array of other entrepreneurial jobs that are low carbon that range from the most cutting-edge atomic technology to Bosom-milk that has been modified," According to the study. The company was founded in the year 2015 . It was founded by Bill Gates. Ginkgo Bioworks is a biotech company that received $350 million of adventure capital in the year 2019, mostly from Gates venture company, Cascade Investment. Luminous Computing is a company that designs neuromorphic photonic integrated circuits to increase AI speed.

In the words of Gates, Mologic, a British health-related innovation company which Gates purchased along with his Soros Economic Development Fund, "has created 10-minute Covid stream tests that are sidelong which they expect to complete only $1," According to Gates.

Chapter 6: Energy And The Environment

According to Gates his report, environmental change and accessibility to electricity are two major interconnected issues. Based on recent technological advances and technological advances, well-known scientists have urged governments as well as the private industry to put their money into standard research and development strategies to lower the cost of obtaining flawless reliable, safe energy. Gates believes that advancements in the field of controlled energy innovations could decrease the flow of ozone-depleting substances and poverty and increase financial returns by stabilizing the cost of energy. "If I were given the option of choosing between the next 10 presidents or making sure that energy is environmentally green and just a fifth expensive, I'd go with the energy option." The president of the United States in 2015 weighed in on the challenges of changing the energy structure of the world away from the use of petroleum derivatives and towards alternative energy sources that are economically viable. Changes in energy sources at a global level typically take a long time. "I admit that we could achieve this faster due to the speed of improvement is increasing and because we've never had a compelling need to switch from one energy source to another" he stated.

According Gates Gates, this dramatic change is contingent on increased funding from the government for vital exploration as well as financially risky private-area investments to facilitate the development of a range of sectors, including thermal power, storage of energy in the network as well as a higher utilization of wind and sunlight-based energy sources, in addition to sunlight-driven fuels. Gates was the driving force behind two campaigns was announced during his 2015 United Nations Climate Change Conference in Paris. One of the campaigns was Mission Innovation where 20 governments agreed to increase their investment in innovative technologies that are free of carbon in 5 years. The other initiative involved Breakthrough Energy, a group of investors who pledged to invest in the development of high-risk renewable energy businesses.

Breakthrough Energy received an additional $1 billion from Gates who had previously given 1 billion in his personal funds to companies in the field of energy innovation. By the end of December Gates directed his US the federal government prepare the groundwork for clean energy research that is similar to that conducted by the National Institutes of Health. Gates has also encouraged wealthy nations to shift to 100 percent engineered beef production to cut down on the amount of ozone depleting substances released in food production. Gates has been accused of holding a large stake within Signature Aviation, a company which operates high-end private planes. He began stripping petroleum derivatives in 2019.

He doesn't believe that divestment will be a positive effects on its own However, he believes that if his attempts to give options do not succeed and he doesn't want to make money from an increase in non-renewable fuel price of the source stock. Following the publication of his book How to Prevent a Climate Emergency Gate's method was criticised as mechanical solutions by environmentalists of the region. Gates' TerraPower and Warren Buffett's PacifiCorp have announced the first sodium-based atomic reactor located in Wyoming on June 20, 2021. The Governor Mike Gordon of Wyoming praised the development as a move towards creating a carbon negative force atomic.

Wyoming Senator John Barrasso, likewise, stated that it may have helped boost the state's productive uranium mining industry.

Chapter 7: Charity

The Bill and Melinda Gates Foundation is a non-profit foundation created through Bill Gates and Melinda Gates. It was founded in 1994. Gates committed a percentage of Microsoft shares to establish the "William H. Gates Foundation," in the spirit of Andrew Carnegie and John D. Rockefeller. in 2000, Gates as well as his other half-half joined three family foundations and Gates gave $5 billion of stock to form the benevolent Bill and Melinda Gates Foundation and is ranked as the globe's most affluent charity according to the Funds for NGOs organization in 2013. The foundation's resources are valued at over $34.6 billion.

Some other notable altruistic organizations, such as for instance the Wellcome Trust, do not permit donors to access data which reveals how their donation is spent, like they do with the foundation. Gates also donated the sum of $20 million Carnegie Mellon University through his foundation to build a new building, known as the Gates Center for Computer Science that was inaugurated in 2009.

According to Gates David Rockefeller's generosity and generous giving was an enormous influence. Gates and his father had meetings with Rockefeller numerous times. their work for charity is not depicted in the Rockefeller family's extraordinary concentration and determination to tackle global issues that other organizations and governments do not see. Bill Gates and Melinda Gates were the second-most liberal Philanthropists of America 2007 contributing nearly $28 billion in donations to charities and plan to donate 95 percent of their wealth to charitable causes in the near future.

The Global Development Division, Global Health Division, United States Division and the Global Policy and Advocacy Division are the five regions of program which make up the organisation. It is a provider of a broad range of general health programs, which include assistance in fighting infectious diseases such as AIDS, TB, and jungle fever and also extensive vaccination campaigns to eliminate the spread of polio. It also provides resources for libraries and educational institutions in addition to college scholarships. In order to provide affordable sterilization facilities in the poorest nations the organization created the water, disinfection as well as cleaning service. It has a stake with its International Rice Research Institute. The institute assists them to help a non-profit organization that is dedicated to making additional vitamin A available to people in the people in the developing world by providing the pro-vitamin "Golden Rice" version. The rice has 50 many times the amount of beta carotene as conventional varieties. The goal of the foundation is to provide high-quality information and services for prophylactic use to over 120 million young and females in the world's poorest regions with the long-term aim of gaining broad acceptance for free family planning. The Los Angeles Times chastised the foundation when it was criticized in 2007 to invest in organizations who have been accused of destabilizing poverty, pollution and pharmaceutical companies that don't offer assistance to nations in need.

Although the group released a report on its investments to evaluate social responsibility, the survey was removed and replaced with an approach of giving the greatest return and making use of the right to vote to influence organizational practices. On the 8th of December in 2020, at the Singapore FinTech Festival, Gates delivered a fireside talk about the topic "Building infrastructure to Support Resilience What the COVID-19 Response has to Learn from the COVID-19 Response on how to Increase Financial Inclusion" and was hosted by anchorperson and writer Shereen Bhan.

Governments have been put in place to safeguard its citizens. In the wake of the COVID-19 virus many tasks were not completed. We should be aware that another epidemic is likely to occur and we need to dedicate resources to be prepared for it, but also realizing that we weren't prepared. We should contribute-similar as having an local unit of firefighters-a bit of money to replicate what could happen and ensure that we're prepared.

COVID - According to Gates the masks that he has 19 ought to be standardized. In an October gathering in 2020 "How can these folks differ from nudists? According to the document, Salwen revealed how he was able to sell his home at $400,000 and donated the majority of it to charities. According to Gates his view the donation was a remarkable charitable gesture from the family since they were not obliged to donate any money; however , she says that people generally should follow the example set by their actions and give back as a top priority in their lives. On the 9th of December, 2010, Bill and Melinda Gates along with the financial patron Warren Buffett, welcomed Joan Salwen to Seattle to discuss the actions of the family did and then on the 9th of December the 9th of December, the entire family took their names to the "Giving Pledge," which promises each to donate a half of their money to a noble cause provided that everything goes as planned.

Personal Donations

There's more than just money has been donated by Bill Gates, but personal gifts as well. For example, the year 1999. Bill Gates donated $20 million to the Massachusetts Institute of Technology for the building of an computer lab. He was aware of how in the past the computers of their lab were. In his words in the moment: "If you look at MIT it's one of our very first partners, and they were awarded technologically the equivalent of El Camino Real status." The new facility will be constructed using concrete with a new structural formula and will function as an opportunity for collaboration between students as well as professors who might face difficulties working in tandem when creating software. Although Microsoft had recently offered financial support to the institution but this was Gates his first donation of his own.

The Maxwell Dworkin Laboratory at John A. Paulson School of Engineering and Applied Sciences (SEAS) is named for the mother of Bill Gates, the founder of Microsoft as well as Steve Ballmer, the former CEO of Microsoft. Each of Bill Gates and Steve Ballmer have contributed generously to the building of this laboratory. Gates also donated $6 million towards the building of the Gates Computer Science Building on the Stanford University campus, which was completed in the month of January in 1996. It houses the Computer Science Department and the Computer Systems Laboratory (CSL) of Stanford's Engineering division are housed in the building.

Gates along with his foundation has been studying global issues related to sterilization since. They have, for instance, covered an event called the (Reinvent the Challenge to Clean Up) that attracted a lot of attention from the media. The year 2014 was the first time Gates consumed water "delivered by the excrement of humans" it was produced by a sewage treatment process called The Omni Processor to bring concerns to light regarding the issue of disinfection as well as possible arrangements. Gates also appeared as a guest on The Tonight Show with Jimmy Fallon in mid-2015, encouraging to taste the different between recycled water and water filtered.

Gates announced on November 17, 2017 he'd contribute fifty million dollars towards the Dementia Discovery Fund, an investment fund that aims to find the cure of Alzheimer's. Gates also pledged another $50 million for studies into Alzheimer's disease. Bill Gates and Melinda Gates have stated that they will leave 10 million dollars to each of their children in the form of an inheritance. With only $30 million left in the bank, they're expected to give away 99.96 percentage of their wealth. On August 25, 2018, Bill Gates allocated $600,000 through his foundation to UNICEF that is helping flooding victims from Kerala, India.

Noble Sports Events Cause Noble.

On the 29th of April 2017 Gates collaborated together with Swiss legendary tennis player Roger Federer in playing in the Match for Africa 4, the non-competitive tennis event at the fully-filled Key Arena in Seattle. The event was held on the occasion that of Roger Federer Foundation's charity efforts in Africa. Federer and Gates took on John Isner, the highest-level American player, as well as Mike McCready, the lead guitarist of Pearl Jam. The duo dominated the game six games to four. The overall goal was to raise $2 million to help children in Africa. The following season, Gates and Federer got back together for their first Match for Africa 5 on March 5, 2018 in the San Jose's SAP Center. Jack Sock, one of the top American players and a formidable copy hammer champion, along with Savannah Guthrie, a co-anchor for the NBC's Today program was their opponent. In a 6-3 win, Gates and Federer won their second game together and the tournament brought in the sum of $2.5 million.

Chapter 8: Works Of Literature

Gates is among the most powerful individuals around the globe. He has published three novels: The Road Ahead, published in November 1995, co-written with Microsoft Chief Executive Officer Nathan Myhrvold and writer Peter Rinearson The book outlined the effects of the explosion of personal computers and portrayed a future that was drastically altered by the rise of a global superhighway for data. A Business at the Speed of Thought was published in 1999. It examines how innovation and business are interconnected and how computerized frameworks and organizations can aid businesses in gaining an advantage in the marketplace.

How to avoid the possibility of a Climate Disaster (February 2021) summarise the lessons Gates learned over a long time of studying environmental changes and investing into solutions to environmental problems. The guidelines to avoid the occurrence of a Climate Disaster (February 2021) provide a summary of the lessons Gates gained during a long time of studying environmental changes and investing funds in the solution of environmental problems.

Wealth matters.

As of 1999, the overflow outspread US $111 billion. In the years since 2000, the value for the Microsoft property has dipped due to the fall in the cost of Microsoft's stock after the bubble burst on the internet as well as the multi-billion-dollar gifts that he's made to his charitable foundations. In May 2006 when asked if he wanted to be the wealthiest person in the world, Gates replied: "I would like to be rich because that would mean I'd have lots of money. But that's not what the point is. There's no place in the world where wealth is that important" and in March of 2010 Gates was ranked second according to Bloomberg's Billionaires List after being displaced for a few times from the list by Carlos Slim. The list was updated in July 2012. Gates came in at third place, just after Amancio Ortega as well as Warren Buffett. In March 2014 Forbes announced the fact that Bill was Microsoft's top shareholder, with 555 million shares, which is 6.4 percent of all outstanding shares, valued at $13.1 billion US dollars. There's lots. Bloomberg Billionaires List listed Bill Gates as the second-highest billionaire in 2010, with an estimated net worth 40 billion. He was was named as the planet's wealthiest individual in Forbes which estimated his net worth in the range of $77.5 billion. Amazon CEO Jeff Bezos briefly surpassed Gates on the 27th of October in 2017 but an hour afterward Gates took the lead back and has not been challenged since "I've made more money than any other person has ever and, happily I've paid more than six billion dollars in tax," Gates told the BBC. Gates is a vocal advocate of higher taxes, especially on wealthy people.

For 18 of the past twenty-four years Bill Gates has topped the Forbes list of billionaires around the world. Apart from Microsoft, Gates owns a handful of assets, among them one which gave him US $616,667 as a salary and the US $30,000 bonus from 2006 that totaled US $966,667. Gates founded Corbis, an advanced imaging business in 1989. The year 2004 was the time he was on the top management staff in Berkshire Hathaway, the trading business run by his long-time companion Warren Buffett. Gates was named an entrepreneur on Forbes' 400 richest people in America release in 1987. considered to be worth $1.25 billion at the time and was also the youngest tycoon in the world. Gates has been listed as a member of Forbes' The World's Billionaires list since 1987. He was also the most wealthy person between 1995 and 1996, 1998 , 2007 and 2009, and up to 2018 after which he was beaten by Jeff Bezos. From 1993 to 2009, and from 2014 until 2017 Gates was the first to be listed on his Forbes 400 rundown. Times selected Gates and his wife, Melinda, and U2's principal entertainer, Bono, as the 2005 People of the Year. The year 2006 was the first time he was cast 7th on the list of "Holy people of Our Time." Gates was listed on The London Sunday Times power list in 1999. He was named the year's CEO from chief executive Officers magazine in 1994, was named number one among the Time's Best 50 Cyber Elite in 1998, and was ranked second on The Upside Elite 100 of every

1999, and was also named as one in the "Best 100 most influential people in the media" in 2001 by The Guardian. in 1996 Gates got inducted into the US National Academy of Engineering for his contribution to the creation and development of human computer technology. In 1998 the American Library Association designated him as an honorary member. He was chosen from the Chinese Academy of Engineering by an unidentified individual.

In the report by Forbes, Gates was ranked as the fourth-highest-powered person worldwide in 2012, a jump from the fifth position in 2011. He was awarded The British Computer Society's 10th Distinguished Fellow in 1994. (DFBCS). Gates was awarded the President's Medal from the New York Institute of Technology in 1999. Gates was awarded honorary doctorates from Nyenrode Business University (2003), KTH Royal Institute of Technology (2002), Waseda University (2005), Tsinghua University (2007), Harvard University (2007) and The Karolinska Institute (2007) along with Cambridge University (2007).

In the same year, he also appointed a trustee privileged for Peking University.

In 2005 the Queen Elizabeth II designated in 2005 Queen Elizabeth II Gates as an honorary knight commander of the Order of the British Empire (KBE). In January 2006, Presidency of Portugal, Jorge Sampaio, conferred on him the Grand Cross of the Order of Prince Henry. He was presented with the Placard of the Order of the Aztec Eagle in November 2006, together with his spouse, Melinda, who was presented with the insignia of the same post for their tireless activities throughout the globe in the field of health and education especially in Mexico specifically through the program "Un not a lot of lectores." In recognition of his accomplishments in Microsoft and for his charitable endeavors, Gates received the Franklin Institute's 2010 Bower Award for Business Leadership.

Additionally to that, The Boy Scouts of America honored him with the Silver Buffalo Award, the most prestigious award for adults from the organization in 2010 for his dedication to young people. Bill Gates and Melinda Gates have been credited for their charitable activities that others in their position couldn't or wouldn't do. They've also been honored with top accolades for their charitable work including being awarded an award called the Jefferson Award for Outstanding Public Service to the Disadvantaged in 2002. In 2006, the Tech Awards presented them with the James C. Morgan Global Humanitarian Award in 2006. Gates as well as his spouse Melinda were awarded his wife Melinda the Padma Bhushan, India's third-highest civilian award in 2015 for their contributions to philanthropy to the nation.

Barack Obama honored Bill and Melinda with the Presidential Medal of Freedom for their charitable activities in the year 2016. Francois Hollande was able to honor Bill as well as Melinda with France's most prestigious honour The Commandant of the Legion of Honor in the next year. In 1997 the flower fly, Eristalis gatesi was named in honor of Bill Gates by entomologists.

Films

Films that comprise components 1999 Pirates of Silicon Valley A film about Microsoft's rise and Apple's rise between the mid-1970s and 1997. Anthony Michael Hall plays Bill Gates. 2002: Not So Strange, a mockumentary about Bill Gates' death on the cutting-edge. Gates was performed in the film by Steve Sires, makes a brief appearance at the premiere. The Social Network, a film that explores the rise of Facebook was released in the year 2010. Steve Sires plays Bill Gates. 2015. Steve Jobs vs. Bill Gates: The Battle for Control of the Personal Computer From 1974 until 1999 The film is a National Geographic Channel original film for the American Genius series.

Film clips and clips

The Macintosh pre-dispatch party in 1983 Steve Jobs had Bill Gates as a participant in The Macintosh match-making game (with Steve Jobs and Mitch Kapor in reference to the TV show, The Dating Game). Steve Jobs with Bill Gates in 2007. All Things Digital, 2009 Gates has given a variety of TED talks on subjects including education, progress and fighting global health issues.

Radio

Bill Gates recently participated in an interview on the radio station BBC in which he spoke about some of his best moments. Bill talks about the relationship he had and friendship with Steve Jobs, meeting Melinda Ann French and the way in which the two of them decided to set up the company they both own. Bill chose "Blue Skyes" from Willie Nelson for music, "The Better Angels of The Nature" written by Steven Pinker for a book as well as an item of extravagance DVD Collection of Lectures by The Teaching Company for extravagance.

TV In the show The Big Bang Theory, Bill Gates appeared as himself. The moment he appeared was appropriately called "The Gates Excited." Additionally, he appeared in an appearance in the final episode of Silicon Valley in 2019. In the Simpsons Episode Das Bus featured Gates as himself.

Chapter 9: A View Of Bill Gates And

Microsoft

Bill Gatedz isn't the only one who's popular with Manu Reorle. In fact, lots of the reorle don't like his music. Perhaps uou are among those. That'dz a dzhame. Bill Gatedz doedz not dedzerve to be slammed. He's incredibly generous and generous. He had a foundation, The Bill and Melinda Gatedz Foundation that was which dzrenddz 1.5 billion dollars in reruears and all of it on the sharitable website saudzedz. The amount is so huge it's difficult to imagine.

In a short time, Bill Gatedz hadz now committed himself to charity work with the hidz foundation full-time. He quit Microsoft to pursue this. Surrridzinglu Reorle, some of them believe that he's an Adzdzhole. They are the people who are jealous, angry and negative about everyone who else's Dzussedzdz. In reality, there is no way that Misrodzoft an rerfest-related company. However, the perfect somranu isn't exidzt! Microsoft is a lot more worse than many somraniedz of corporate Amerisa.

Bill Gates hadz been a incredible dzussedzdz and was extremely generous. There is no reason to feel any sentiments towards the man, other than redzrest and admiration for what he did with nothing using Misrodzoft.

Let's be realistic here. You shouldn't be giving to other people even if you don't have anything. In the event that Bill Gatedz had not started taking money, he would have nothing to offer. Who would have benefitted by his humility instead of a shrewd entrepreneur? Nobody.

Bill Gatedz was smart enough to know the idea. He was a genius and created an organization that was so impressive that it was able to become an actual force to make a difference in the world. Instead of sitting around and muttering about how he made all the money in the world, inquire about what you're doing to help make the world more livable.

Bill Gates is always busy daddy, fighting global hunger, and donating money to AIDS redzearsh and as a general actor who is believed to help anyone.

You do not hurt uourdzelf when uou take advantage of otherdz' success. If you think that the rich Reorle are rish and that they are greedy and arrogant how does that affect on your chances of becoming wealthy? If you believe you're a decent rerdzon, and rish folks aren't good Reorle, you aren't likely to turn into a the rish.

2.2 The Beginning of the Business

Many ways in order to be able to understand the origins of Misrodzoft it is necessary to be aware of Bill Gatedz's earlu exrodzure to the somruterdz. When he was 13 years old, an 8th grader from Lakedzide Prer School situated in Seattle, Wadzhington, he and dzeveral sladzdzmatedz received rare assedzdz by an ASR Teleture terminal that was connected on an unspecified badzidz connected to an GE mainframe. The terminal was then rurshadzed by the Dzshool'dz Mother'dz Club with the proceeds from a rummage sales. It was there that he met his classmates and later co-founder Paul Allen.

The time blosk that was somruter times on the GE the mainframe exhaudzted. A handful of Lakedzide children had become part of the first generation of whiz kiddz early haskerdz with a unique expertise and knowledge of computers of the time. They found a of a rrovider that was used for GE that was part of CCC (Comruter Center Corroration) which gave them a restricted access to the DEC PDP-10 miniaturesomruter. These were the rre PC daudz. There was no way anyone could be able to afford a somruter at home or in their business. In the case of Dztead, they made use of a terminal to remote to a massive fasilitu which provided somruting power for the basis of a fee-per-use.

Bill also had a fascination with computers. Often he would go to CCC in-rerdzon to be able to study the dzourse dzourse on the system and be proficient in the rrogramming language that the da. Gatedz along with Allen were part of four Lakeside children who were barred from CCC for the duration of a whole day when it was discovered that they had used an exrloit within the dzudztem that was in oreration to gain an extra hour of somrutering for no cost of the sharge.

Following the end of the ban four students offered to search for bugs in CCC's software for time. The arrangement continued for two more years, until the year 1970 when CCC was unable to produce the budzinedzdz. Then, in the year 2000 the somranu Information Sciences Inc. hired four of the Lakedzide kids (Bill Gatedz Paul Allen, Ris Weiland as well as Kent Evandz) to write the budzinedzdz Dzoftware. The first project was an rauroll system written in COBOL. The developers were paid royalties in addition to the opportunity to use their somruter time free to work on their project.

In the four ueardz which were radzdzed Bill was 17 when he formed a company along together with Paul Allen called Traf-O-Data. The midzdzion was designed to enhance the performance of traffis and location rlanning engineers by reading raw data from the roadway traffic counters and generating reports called analutisdz that provide insight into the ratterndz of traffis. Traf-O-Data wadzn't a roaring dzussedzdz. Nevertheledzdz and both Gatedz and Allen were later to dzau the to dzeminal as part of the final development of Misrodzoft.

Gates completed his studies at Lakedzide in 1973. He moved away from Seattle for Harvard. Gatedz decided to major in law but enrolled in mathematics and graduate level dzsiense courses. Gatedz was able to demonstrate his extraordinary ability with programming while at Harvard. In his dzesond at the time the algorithm he devised was to solve "ransake sorting" as an answer to the undzolved programming programs which were presented within a combinatorics slidezdz written by the rrofedzdzor Harry Lewis. Gatedz's algorithm dominated the resord as the most efficient verdzion for more than thirty years, and its dzussedzdzor algorithm was fadzter by less than 1percent. The Gatedz dzolution was codified in a rarer publication by collaborating with Harvard Somruter Dzsientidzt Chridztodz Paradimitriou.

While Gatedz and Allen maintained contact throughout the years following (including an internship at Honeuwell during the summer of 1974), Microsoft might never be in existence without a pivotal now-hidztoris Idzdzue in POPULAR Electronics Magazine. The January 1975 sover story was on the

MITS Altair 8800, an imrredzdzive misrorrosedzdzor-badzed somruter aimed at computer hobbyists. The real-world application of a misrorrosedzdzor could be an important game changer and one that Gatedz as well as Allen believed could be revolutionary. Theuisklu put it all together that, with the growth of misrorrosedzdzors, there will be an increasing demand for dzoftware which included rrogramming languagedz as well as business-oriented applications. SOFTware designed for MICROrrosedzdzordz was an innovative idea , and led them to the form MICROSOFT (initiallu named the name MICRO-SOFT) to revive the big idea. The company was officially created on Arril 4 on the 4th of April, 1975.

MITS, makers of the Altair 8800 computer were based in Albu?uer?ue, New Mexico. By November of 1975, Bill and Paul dropped everything and moved to Albu?uer?ue in hopes to get early access to the machine. Gates took a leave of absence from Harvard to work with Allen at MITS. Microsoft became independent of MITS in late 1976 and went on to develop software for various other microprocessor-based computing platforms, including, most notoriously IBM for its IBM PC and Apple for its Mac in the 1980s. On New Year's Day of January 1979, Microsoft left Albu◌uer◌ue for good, establishing a new head◌uarters in Bellvue, Washington where it would remain until February 26, 1986, at the completion of Microsoft's famous Redmond, Washington corporate campus at "One Microsoft Way." Weeks later, on March 13, 1986, Microsoft became public, creating epic wealth for the company's founders and staff.

His Career From the Start to Now

Bill Gates' leadership style is a very participative one hence when there is participation, motivation is increased. Bill Gates understood what it takes to motivate his employees so all of them were engaged, enthusiastic and excited about their work. Bill Gates is a very flexible person and he recognized his role to be the visionary of the company. He is a task motivated leader and a role model to all his co-workers in which his enthusiasm, hard-working nature and judgment skills would motivate his staff and involve his friends to work with him.

Besides that, Microsoft provides worker benefits such as the inclusion of health benefits, transportation, food availability, child care benefits, and other essential discounts. He believed that employee ownership was critical in increasing employee motivation and retention hence, he offered his employees with rewards such as high salaries and equity. With all of these benefits done to impress the employees of Microsoft, Gates believed that the employees would be motivated to do their work.

Other than that, Gates understands that leadership isn't all about control, it's about trusting and respecting others, which makes the employees feel more appreciated and loyalty which would motivate the employees to work better in the workplace.

Success Strategy of Bill Gates As Small Business Entrepreneur For Your Own Home Business

Strategies are strategies. Dismiss for a moment from your mind what some people are saying about Bill Gates's offensive practices he used to transform himself from a small business entrepreneur to a titan in the business world. There are yet honest-to-goodness strategies we can glean from his sleeves. We can study, learn from them and possibly apply them in our own home-based business. Upon this premise that this book was written.

The strategy of Bill Gates – "Have a Vision"

Bill Gates used the same strategy to jump-start his small business to today's business behemoth. Based on research, the strategy of Bill Gates is grounded upon the following:

"Have a VISION of what you want to achieve and hold on to that vision come wrath or high water."

His vision was:

"A Personal Computer on every desk."

Almost everybody is familiar about how once upon a time the small business entrepreneur Bill Gates secured mighty IBM's contract to supply the latter's operating system. When he was negotiating with the IBM people, he had no operating system as yet. He was able to buy a Disk Operating System or DOS for $50 thousand. In the end, he got the contract. Why?

Bill Gates was guided by his vision - that every desk all over the world should have a computer on it. This vision enabled him to provide IBM with a DOS operating system and have control over it including to whom he wanted it sold to.

Beginning an Entrepreneur

Before he became an entrepreneur, Bill Gates had nurtured the vision that software will one day rule the world. During high school, he spent many late nights with friend Paul Allen tinkering with the school's computer system.

He dropped out of college after completing his junior year at Harvard. Instead, he and his bosom friend Paul Allen set up a small business - a software company - in faraway New Mexico. This move was in accordance with his vision.

His vision became clearer as he moved from a total newbie to one with small business to keep. His vision was clothed in clearer terms, as he negotiated the DOS deal with IBM.

Better Late than Never

Bill Gates's company ultimately became the leader in the software arena. During the first half of the 1990's - 1993 to be exact - he was among the last of the software titans to acknowledge the future significance of the Internet.

But once he did realize that indeed the Internet was the wave of the future, he had the tenacity to reshape his vision. His vision retained its old flavor - that is, software dominance in commerce, industry and in every field. It was rehashed in his own words as follows:

"In the years ahead, the Internet will have an even more profound effect on the way we work, live and learn ... this technology will be one of the key cultural and economic forces of the early 21st century."

At this moment in time, Bill Gates is guided by the vision that the Internet is the wave of the present and the foreseeable future.

Lessons Learned

You can learn from Bill Gates by having your own vision for your small business. Lay down this vision in your mind. Then put it into writing. Read your vision every day while at work in your small corner of the house. Your vision could be as short-term as the following:

"To make my web site land within the top five of Google when people search for the keywords 'home based business,'" or "$200,000 earning this year from Google Adsense," or "To enrich the content of my web site using the theme 'scrap bookmaking.'"

Do not limit yourself to short-term vision. Aim for the long-term. A five to ten years period would suffice. Technology may change but your vision will essentially be the same. You may refine it if deemed necessary, like incorporating the effect of technological changes - as Bill Gates did.

Your Share of the Pie

Everybody - from Bill Gates down to your entrepreneur friend - has recognized the tremendous role of the Internet in business developments. Some of the more immediate pressing concerns you should consider at this stage concerning your home based business are the following:

•   General preference for digital transactions by clients. For example, as a beginning Internet entrepreneur, you should meet your clients' demands who favor the use of an online payment system.

•   Choose products that are preferred by people at this time when the Internet is dominating people's lives. It has been determined that information products and web shopping are favored by most consumers. Information products include your very own ebooks and "how-to" manuals.

- Make it your aim that your products are cheap, very useful, and the best among the rest of competing products. This applies most especially to shopping products. For your own digital products, you have the advantage of pricing them according to your own estimation.

You as the author of your own digital product determines the price level. It is no wonder why gurus like Jay Abraham, Jim Daniels, and the late Corey Rudl have become so wealthy from selling their own digital pieces.

As for these three gurus, they will be among the titans that we will tackle in future issues of this series.

How Smart Bill Gate Is

Intelligence is notoriously difficult to define and measure, but without a doubt, Bill Gates is on the 'fairly high' end of most metrics. But he does have some serious lapses in understanding.

Intelligence has different dimensions. Bill Gates is the richest man in the world, so he must have a great deal of practical intelligence. In terms of academic intelligence, he is certainly not among the top 1% technically skilled people in the world, as there is no technology that he himself has innovated. Also in terms of business acumen or a visionary, his statistics reveal more luck than extraordinary talent. See how many opportunities has missed. After Windows and Office, MS has produced no other breakthrough technology. They missed on the browser, they missed on social networking, and most recently missed on handheld revolution. Around the year 2000, someone wrote an op-ed in WSJ where he predicted the end of the road for PC, and the very next day Bill Gates challenged the original article by his own op-ed where he insisted that the PC revolution was just beginning.

Any intelligence Bill Gates may have had in the past has been eclipsed by his utter disastrous statements he has recently made. So, the question is how intelligent is Bill Gates.

"The Private sector is inept" is an example of an outrageous statement. History is on my side that governments across the board have shown themselves to be by far more inept at everything they touch. He went on to say that Socialism was the only answer to stopping Global warming.

And so what if the Private sector inept? Capitalist put their own money at risk to achieve a financial gain. If they fail, who loses? Only the Capitalists lose. On the other hand, government ineptness (such as Solyndra to start with) puts all of our money at risk with devastating results when they think they know best what to do with our sacred money.

Gates can point to wonderful things that business and government alliances or government special groups have wrought that have been to the betterment of mankind. But it is complete nonsense to think none of this would have been developed in the absence of government handouts. Also, many of the technologies are developed for the inevitable use in or as weapons of war.

And many of the business/government alliances have ended tragically for people.

One only has to turn the pages back to the use of chemical warfare used in WWI to see the ugliness that business/government bonds can create.

And those in the anti-nuclear bomb crowd would be on the moral high ground to point to the fact it was the government that created the nuclear bomb. Yes, it ended the war with Japan and saved many American/Allied lives. But we now live in an age where even the smallest country (aka Iran) is determined to have one. What kind of world will it be like 20 years from now when Iran, then Saudi Arabia, then maybe Jordan and others have The Bomb? Can we even imagine such a place?

Bill Gates started the foundation that bears his and his wife's name. This was an utterly disastrous idea. Mark my words: when he is dead and gone, its mission statement will morph into something that will go beyond whatever it is now. History, yet again, is replete with foundations that have drifted far from their original intent. The most famous one being the Ford Foundation. Henry Ford II resigned from the foundation had become frustrated and watching its drift toward socialism. If Bill Gates thinks that what he has established will spearhead us to a greater future after he is dead. He will weep in his grave.

These Leftist leaning foundations wield more power in setting government policy than they should have ever been allowed to have. Common Core is a grand example of this.

Gates would have done immeasurably better by taking his billions, investing them in manufacturing which, by the way, during his reign pulled up stakes and left this country. And as the USA is not just wading into an ocean of Socialism but has dived straight into it, we see the incomes of people whher away ensuring our drift into 3rd Worldism. Thanks for nothing, Bill.

And finally, his belief that government is the Great White Hope for stopping Global Warming, is an utterly appalling and amazingly stupid statement that will end up haunting him for the rest of his days.

Proof that Bill Gates Is Intelligent -

- When Mainframe computer was launched in early 1980's Bill Gates learnt all about it just by reading it's manuals and was also able to develop Tic Tac Toe in a few months (just by reading his manual). Now people are not able to learn programming even after taking programming classes, using the internet, etc and he learned all Mainframe computer just by reading it's manuals. Also programming languages nowadays simpler as compared to languages used in the early 1980s.

• Bill Gates wrote software for his school when he was just a Kid which made him 🮲uite popular in his school.

• His IQ is 160 more than a normal person

As a student at Harvard in the 1970s, Bill Gates impressed more than one faculty member with his mathematical brilliance. He proposed an elegant solution to what's known as "pancake sorting," and his insights were published in the journal Discrete Mathematics in 1979, in a paper co-bylined with then Harvard professor Christos Papadimitriou.

A few years ago, Papadimitriou, now a professor of computer science at the

University of California, Berkeley, shared an anecdote about working with Gates in a publication of the Association for Computing Machinery.

The story serves as a reminder that the wealthiest and most successful people among us may have been exceptional from the start.

Here's Papadimitriou:

When I was an assistant professor at Harvard, Bill was a junior. My girlfriend back then said that I had told her: "There's this undergrad at school who is the smartest person I've ever met."

That semester, Gates was fascinated with a math problem called pancake sorting: How can you sort a list of numbers, say 3-4-2-1-5, by flipping prefixes of the list? You can flip the first two numbers to get 4-3-2-1-5, and the first four to finish it off: 1-2-3-4-5. Just two flips. But for a list of n numbers, nobody knew how to do it with fewer than $2n$ flips. Bill came to me with an idea for doing it with only $1.67n$ flips. We proved his algorithm correct, and we proved a lower bound-it cannot be done faster than $1.06n$

flips. We held the record in pancake sorting for decades. It was a silly problem back then, but it became important because human chromosomes mutate this way.

Two years later, I called to tell him our paper had been accepted to a fine math journal. He sounded eminently disinterested. He had moved to Albuquerque, New Mexico to run a small company writing code for microprocessors, of all things. I remember thinking: "Such a brilliant kid. What a waste."

Thirty years later, other researchers found a sorting strategy that's 1% faster. But according to an NPR interview with Harry Lewis, another Harvard professor who taught Gates in the 1970s, those researchers had the help of powerful computers. The young Gates, on the other hand, relied solely on his own cognitive resources (and in fact, he helped develop the computers that would find a faster solution).

It's easy to dismiss these reminiscences as exceptions to the rule - the rule that anyone can make it big without being a genius at age 20.

But a growing body of research suggests that intelligence is a remarkably good predictor of wealth and success later in life.

Test

Your test performance at a young age may predict your wealth and success later in life.

In 2013, Jonathan Wai, a professor at Duke University's Talent Identification Program, published a study that found the majority of Fortune 500 CEOs and billionaires had attended an elite academic institution either as an undergraduate or graduate student, putting them in the top 1% of cognitive ability. Even among the top 0.0000001% of the wealth, Wai reported, those who earned more were generally better educated.

More recent research by Wai has found that about 40% of a sample of 1,991 CEOs attended elite schools, which presumably means they were in the top 1% of cognitive ability. Moreover, Wai found that companies run by more highly-educated

CEOs tended to perform better. Wai evaluates admission to an elite institution with smarts because those schools admit only students with top SAT scores and SAT scores are generally related to intelligence.

Wai's methodology and conclusions have been criticized, for example by Steve Siebold, author of "How Rich People Think," and Wai admits that he would have preferred to gain access to people's SAT scores if that were possible. In an article on Business Insider, Wai acknowledged, "It might be that the power of the networks, brand name, and quality of education that come with elite school attendance is why so many of these people ended up in such positions of influence."

Another small study, conducted by researchers at Vanderbilt University, found that 320 students who had scored above the 1 in 10,000 level on the SAT before age 13 held more prestigious jobs at more prestigious companies by age 38 than the average population.

Bill Gates himself has acknowledged the potential link between intelligence and professional success. In 2005, he told Forbes: "Microsoft must win the IQ war, or we won't have a future."

That intelligence might play more than a minimal role in individual success is an uncomfortable idea to consider. But the takeaway from these studies and anecdotes isn't that, if you aren't off-the-charts intelligent (at least by standard measures of intelligence), you can't or won't get anywhere.

What Motivates Bill Gates to Become Successful

What motivates Bill Gates is an intense desire to do well. His parents contributed to the development of that attitude by organizing all sorts of competitive games for the family, when Bill was young.

This letter from Bill and Melinda Gates explains it all:

"Our friend and co-trustee Warren Buffett once gave us some great advice about philanthropy: "Don't just go for safe projects," he said. "Take on the really tough problems."

We couldn't agree more. Our foundation is teaming up with partners around the world to take on some tough challenges: extreme poverty and poor health in developing countries, and the failures of America's education system. We focus on only a few issues because we think that's the best way to have great impact, and we focus on these issues in particular because we think they are the biggest barriers that prevent people from making the most of their lives.

For each issue we work on, we fund innovative ideas that could help remove these barriers: new techniques to help farmers in developing countries grow more food and earn more money; new tools to prevent and treat deadly diseases; new methods to help students and teachers in the classroom. Some of the projects we fund will fail. We not only accept that, we expect it—because we think an essential role of philanthropy is to make bets on promising solutions that governments and businesses can't afford to make. As we learn which bets pay off, we have to adjust our strategies and share the results so everyone can benefit.

We're both optimists. We believe by doing these things—focusing on a few big goals and working with our partners on innovative solutions—we can help every person get the chance to live a healthy, productive life."

Out of the dorms of Harvard and into the secluded world of digital-technology geeks and the magic of coding. Genius tech architect, an influential global leader and crusader of the greatest revolution in philanthropy. The 'impatient optimist', Bill Gates.

"I can do anything I put my mind into." Those were the prophetic words of a young boy, aged 11 - William Henry Gates III. A non-conformist, intellectual introvert and a deep thinker. In childhood dreams, it was not ever Land he inhabited, but the burning battlefields of the legendary French emperor Napoleon, one of his heroes. His brain was wired for games of strategy and thrived out of the intense thrill of risk. Young Bill was famed for his strong persistence, fiery ambition and fierce spirit of competition. And, keeping the goal to win always in sight.

"I really had a lot of dreams when I was a kid, and I think a great deal of that grew out of the fact that I had a chance to read a lot."

The world of visionary imagination stems from the expansion of perception outside the limits of conventional knowledge. One of the most pronounced qualities of Gates is his discerning passion for lifelong learning. From the adventures of Tarzan and Martian stories of Edgar Rice Burroughs to futuristic and science-fiction books of Isaac Asimov, biographies of famous men that left their mark in the history, along with Freud's masterpieces of psychoanalytic theories. These were among the first intriguing readings that shaped the beautifully complex mind of Bill Gates.

"Be nice to nerds. Chances are you'll end up working for one." A self-confessed math geek with a passion for coding, at the age of 13, Gates wrote his first computer program - a point in his life that he always proudly treasures. The sparkle of high achievement was vivid, even back then. Years later, remembering his best childhood friend, he would reveal one small thread of the beginnings of his epic career: "We read Fortune together. We were going to conquer the world."

High on the energy of big dreams, he placed a challenging bet - one day, he would indeed conquer the whole world! Life loves the daring ones, and so Gates went ahead to win with vengeance. After a few rebel days and sleepless nights at Harvard, he left it all behind to free his mind into what he truly loved, becoming the most famous and wildly successful Harvard dropout in the history of the entrepreneurial world.

The Microsoft real giant software company was formed in 1975. Its abbreviation is microcomputer software. It soon became popular and went on to completely change the way people use computers.

The company helped to make the computer easier to the users with its developing and purchasing software and made it a commercial success. The big success of Microsoft began with the MS-DOS computer operating system and Bill Gates licensed it to IBM. Gates also set protecting the royalties and he could acquire from computer software by fighting against all forms of software piracy.

At age 25, Gates obliged IBM to let him keep the proprietary rights to the DOS operating system they had him develop for a program called the pc. Actually, he purchased the program from other company and modifying for the PC. Thinking the program would be ꆛuickly replaced anyway, IBM agreed to pay for a license to use it rather than purchasing it outright. Now Microsoft software operates 90 percent of the world's desktop computers.

Microsoft launched Windows 1.0 in 1983, which produced a graphical user interface better graphics and multitasking. After five years Microsoft reproduced a number of windows versions which added many programs, flexibility, and character. When Microsoft grew, the share price goes to the mountain, and Bill Gates became the youngest billionaire at the age of 31 in the USA.

In 1990 Microsoft actually organized by Bill Gates made a new version of Windows named Windows 3.0 with an improved graphics and features and it sold 10 million copies or more. After followed by Windows 3.1, 3.11 Microsoft added networking support. On the success of that type of OS Microsoft developed Windows 95 and upgraded the new windows 98, windows 98se, windows 2000, Millennium Edition, Windows XP, Windows Vista and the latest version Windows 7. While innovative windows came out Microsoft take market share more and along with their popular software such as Office, games, etc has seen Gates become the richest man in the world and his estimated property US$46 billion.

Gates also has interests not only computer software but also in other business. He has many investments as including Corbis Corporation, Berkshire Hathaway Inc, Teledesic Corporation.

Being the richest man in the world Bill Gates created one of the world's largest charity90. The Bill and Melinda Gates Foundation donates totally more than $1 billion every year. The foundation was formed in 2000 after merging the Gates Learning Foundation and William H. Gates Foundation. The aim is to bring innovations in health and learning to the global community.

From the foundation in 1975 until 2006, Gates had a major task for the corporation product strategy. He effectively launches the various type of products, and as a result, Microsoft attained a dominant position.

Hence Gates is an executive. Met randomly with the senior managers and program managers. Gates's responsibility at Microsoft for most of its history was mainly a management and executive role. However, he was an active software developer in previous years. He was officially been on a development team since working on the TRS-80 Model 100 line, but wrote code as late as 1989 that launched in the company's products. On June 15, 2006, Gates told that he would transition out of his day-to-day role over the next two years to dedicate more time to philanthropy. He divided his responsibilities between two successors, placing Ray Ozzie in charge of day-to-day management and Craig Mundie in charge of long-term product strategy.

Bill Gates is playing a very active role in the workings of the Microsoft Company, but he has handed the position of CEO to Steve Ballmer. Now Gates holds the positions of Chairman and Chief Software Architect. Now His plans to take on fewer workings at Microsoft and try to devote all his time to the Bill and Melinda Gates Foundation.

Time magazine called Gates, one of the 100 most influential people of 2004, 2005, and 2006. Time also collectively named Gates, his wife Melinda and rock band U2's lead singer Bono as the 2005 Persons of the Year for their caring efforts. He got vote eighth in the list of "Heroes of our time" in 2006. In 1999 Gates was listed in the Sunday Times power list. CEO of the year by Chief Executive Officers magazine in 1994, ranked number one in the "Top 50 Cyber Elite" by Time in 1998, ranked number two in the Upside Elite 100 in 1999 and was included in The Guardian as one of the "Top 100 influential people in media" in 2001.

He has taken honorary doctorates from Nyenrode Business Universiteit, Breukelen, The Netherlands, in 2000; the Royal Institute of Technology, Stockholm, Sweden, in 2002; Waseda University, Tokyo, Japan, in 2005; Tsinghua University, Beijing, China, in April 2007; Harvard University in June 2007; the Karolinska Institutet, Stockholm, in January 2008, and Cambridge University in June 2009. He was also an honorary trustee of Peking University in 2007. An honorary Knight Commander of the Order of the British Empire (KBE) by Queen Elizabeth II in 2005 was taken by Bill Gates. Some entomologists name the Bill Gates flower fly, Eristalis gatesi, in his honor.

In November 2006, he and his wife were awarded the Order of the Aztec Eagle for their philanthropic work around the world in the areas of health and education, particularly in Mexico, and specifically in the program "Un país de lectores". In October 2009, it was declared that Gates will be awarded the 2010 Bower Award for Business Leadership of The Franklin Institute for his success in business and for his philanthropic work.

With his great success, it came many criticisms. With his ambitious and aggressive business philosophy, Gates or his Microsoft lawyers are fighting legal battles almost since Microsoft began. Microsoft is dominating every market through acquisition, aggressive business policy or a combination of them. Many of the largest technology companies have fought legally against the actions of Microsoft, including Apple Computer, Netscape, Opera, WordPerfect, and Sun Microsystems. The Creativity. It is common, particularly within the management literature, to associate entrepreneurship with boldness, daring, imagination, or creativity.

These accounts emphasize the personal, psychological features of the entrepreneur. Entrepreneurship, in this conception, is not a required component of all human decision-making, but a specialized activity that some individuals are well able to perform.

If these characteristics are the essence of entrepreneurship, then entrepreneurship has no obvious link to the theory of the firm at least not without further arguments. The necessary personal features can presumably be taken by the contract on the market by buying advising services, project management, and the like. Moreover, the literature does not explain clearly whether imagination and creativity are necessary, sufficient, or incidental conditions for entrepreneurship. Clearly, the founders of many firms are imaginative and creative. Fortunately, Bill Gates has this character and he builds the big software company Microsoft.

Intelligent. He believes that if you are intelligent and know how to apply your intelligence, you can achieve anything. From childhood, Bill was ambitious, intelligent and competitive. These qualities helped him to attain the top position in the profession he chose.

Visionary. Microsoft's vision is "A computer on every desk and Microsoft software on every computer he will continue to stomp out the competition until he dies. Every business and household must have a computer and must run Microsoft software", was the basic guiding vision of Bill Gates.

Passion. When as a student at the Harvard University, every single student would have wanted to be part of the great institute and graduate to be successful, Bill Gates decided to stop studying and pursue his dream of writing software's for every computer in the world

He was just passionate about software, coding, and technology that incidentally also made him the richest man in the world.

5.2 Discover What Bill Gates Had to Say in Front of Thousands of College Kids

Bill Gates said that they should drop out because they still had the time to make something happen with their lives. This is coming from someone who has been able to achieve success by dropping out of college so you know that he knows the truth.

Most of us are lead to believe that in order to be successful in life you have to go to college get good grades in order to get a good job. But the truth is that college only slows the process down because it takes 4 years out of your life and it's pretty much useless. So when you drop out you can invest your time into something that's going to better yourself and is going to increase your education.

So you must understand that the education you need in order to succeed in life is self-education. As you continue to grow and develop you're going to be able to get educated on the different ways to be successful and all you are going to be doing is investing your time. What happened if Bill Gates decided not to dedicate his time to building his business and instead decide to go to college. This is why you must understand that your time is very valuable so you must choose wisely where you want to invest it. Not many people are aware of how valuable their time is and they usually waste it away.

5.3 Bill Gates 4-Point Plan to Solve Complex Problems

In his June 7, 2007 commencement speech delivered at Harvard, Microsoft's Bill Gates has singled out "complexity" as the chief culprit why not only many serious problems around the world don't get solved but also why people don't get involved. If only complex problems could be attacked with a proper methodology then we would have better success at solving global problems like illiteracy, epidemics, lack of clean drinking water, etc. Gates said.

The 4-Point Plan suggested by America's richest businessman and philanthropist involves the following steps:

1.   Determine a goal. What is the desired "end state"?

2.   Find the "highest leverage approach." Which approach would yield the highest result towards the goal?

3.   Discover the ideal technology for that approach.

4. But in the meanwhile, make the smartest application of the existing technology.

Gates explained his ideal approach to eradicate AIDS as an illustration of his 4-Point Plan:

1. The goal is to eradicate AIDS. period.

2. Prevention is the " highest leverage approach" since it brings the highest degree of protection.

3. The ideal technology would be a vaccine that with a single dose would protect people for a lifetime. But that technology is still many years away.

4. Doing the best with the technology we do have involves encouraging people "to avoid risky behavior."

Chapter 10: Bill Gates & Paul Allen - Secrets

Of Legendary Business Partnerships

Through The Eyes Of Numerology

Bill Gates and Paul Allen have a lot more in common than Microsoft according to this character trait analysis based on Numerology. If you like the Discovery Channel and A&E, you will be delighted to learn what Numerology, an ancient science based on mathematics, reveals about the "story BEHIND the story".

Using Numerology to analyze the birth dates of these two childhood friends and now world-famous philanthropists, we find that Bill Gates and Paul Allen ironically share the same Life Path number of 4. And oh, by the way, Oprah is also a 4.

Why is this important? The Life Path number comes from our birth dates and is the single most important number in our Numerology charts because it shines a light on the path that leads to discovering our life purpose and experiencing true fulfillment.

And despite their differences, Bill and Paul were born to walk the same path.

The Upside Of Business Partners Sharing A Four Life Path:

As evidenced by Bill and Paul's common Life Path number of 4, from the start they had inborn tendencies to be practical and down-to-earth individuals with strong ideas about right and wrong. Orderly and organized, systematic and controlled, they are decisive and methodical, employing a step-by-step rational approach to problem-solving.

Once committed, neither of them gives up easily!

And naturally disinterested in 'get rich quick' schemes, they have a higher level of trust in hard work and long hours to establish a solid business foundation. Precise, tenacious and persevering, Bill and Paul were both born with great potential for success, but only the kind of success that comes after putting out massive effort and overcoming the limitations so often encountered on the 4 Life Path.

Thankfully, justice and honesty are sacred to both, so they share a tendency to be naturally reliable and dependable -- virtual cornerstones in their communities.

They are not idealists, but both are willing to work for a better world in a realistic way. Although sometimes a bit rigid in their ideas and too quick in judging others, they are loyal to those they love and tend to work well with others. While being part of a team, however, it is important for them to have their own responsibilities and well-defined tasks since they perform better when their responsibilities do not overlap with those of others.

Both Bill and Paul possess rare discipline and perseverance and not everyone can keep up with them, so they undoubtedly need to exercise caution to avoid being bossy and rude. As travel companions on the 4 Life Path, they have a natural ability to handle money carefully and like the security of nest egg, so it's no coincidence that their mutual love of work led them into a career early in life.

However, due to their shared methodical nature, they can both easily become rigid and stuck in convention. They can also be overly cautious when changes are necessary and this can cause them to miss opportunities that present themselves.

Most 4 Life Paths could use a tad bit more flexibility, but they do tend to be well-suited for marriage and often become responsible, loving parents. However, anything that violates their profound sense of order, such as separation or divorce, can be a shattering experience for them and they can easily become obsessed or even vengeful, seeking their own definition of justice.

In the end, both Bill Gates and Paul Allen are courageous and true survivors. They share the life path of "The Builder". They naturally tend to be the foundation of any enterprise, and their hard work and practical, traditional values pay off to provide them with the rewards they seek and deserve.

The Downside Of This Combination:

There are also some very real challenges in a business relationship where both partners share a four in this part of their charts. The bottom line is this particular combination often produces a relationship that is either excellent or extremely stressful. There is not much middle ground.

The lifestyle requirements of two partners on a 4 Life Path are usually very similar and they both like a certain amount of organization, predictability, and routine in their lives. They don't mind being surprised once in a while, but they do like their daily routines to be firmly established, and preferably not interrupted.

Even aside from their natural compatibility, it would be impossible for partners who share the 4 Life Path to sustain this relationship without making some adjustments. The details are important because both of them tend to get quickly irritated when their carefully established daily routines are disturbed.

It is important that they respect each other's lifestyle and habits and not attempt to sacrifice their own desires to accommodate each other. Instead, they need to arrange a more separate routine and live part of their daily life without much interaction. It is better than trying to adjust to each other, thereby creating small irritations and minor annoyances that over time turn into growing sources of anger.

Bill and Paul are both reliable, dependable people. They honor their promises. This is a powerful ally in their relationship, since it is important for Paul to be able to rely on Bill, and vice versa. However, if taken too far, their grounded, practical natures can also create a somewhat rigid lifestyle that will most likely lead to frustration and gradual alienation from friends and family members.

The Bottom Line:

Lacking tolerance and open-minded acceptance of other people's lifestyles can put a stranglehold on both Bill and Paul's social lives, and indirectly a strain on their own relationship.

Therefore, while other core numbers in their Numerology charts are important to consider as well, the keywords to maintaining a successful relationship between two business partners sharing a 4 Life Path are tolerance and flexibility.

Bill Gates - Being a Giver

Bill Gates is among the most philanthropic men to be found on the face of the planet today. With his foundation called the Bill and Melinda Gates Foundation, he donates more than 1.5 billion dollars each year to the charity. Just pause for a moment and think of this figure, wow!

Remember Bill Gates just tendered his resignation to Microsoft to spend all his time with the Foundation and to give his whole life to the charitable work. This is the kind of guy most would still talk about as an asshole. It must be a case of sour grapes; the unsuccessful people having a negative attitude about Bill Gates. Now you must be wondering if Microsoft is totally unblemished. May be not, but there are likely to be more evil corporate in America.

Generally, Microsoft is respectable and Bill Gates too, and that is why we celebrate his success, achievements, and social activities. He has become a role model to many of how one can climb to great wealth from the scratch.

The bottom line is that one must be a taker before he can become a giver or else there would be nothing to give out. There is no virtue in trying to remain small in order to appear humble.

Maybe Bill Gates had an idea about this and so he tried hard to turn himself into a person who had the capacity to make an impact in the world. If you are just sitting there wondering what your meager savings can do, what about asking yourself what you are doing to make your society better?. What Bill Gates is doing to help the world is huge, ranging from the AIDS research funding, alleviating hunger in the world, and just trying his best to be an excellent person internationally.

There is a wrong attitude in some who tend to think that those who are successful and wealthy are very evil, greedy and selfish people. Such an attitude should be purged from our midst because how will anyone ever aspire to become wealthy if he thinks all the rich people are just evil? It means in his mind he is a good person and so he should just remain poor.

Is Bill Gates Doing More Good When He Keeps His Money Or When He Gives it Away?

The question of whether Bill Gates is doing more good when he keeps his money or when he gives it away is an interesting one. In which of these two scenarios does mankind benefit more? Before you dismiss this as a clearly ridiculous query, one not even worth considering, ponder this.

When you are worth tens of billions of dollars, where do you keep your stash? Do you hide it under your mattress? That would make for a very lumpy sleeping surface; as a billionaire, it's not very likely you would put up with such discomfort.

How about burying your fortune in the backyard? With all that loot, you're not going to be doing any digging. After all, you didn't get rich digging holes in the ground, but rather by using your noodle, and you're not about to start with the manual labor now. You could, however, get the gardener to plant the funds in the Azalea bed, but this might not be such a good idea, either. Not to cast aspersions on landscapers everywhere, but what's to keep her (don't want to be sexist here) from digging up the treasure when you are not around and heading for the South Sea Islands? People with obscene (as some might think) amounts of money (the perspective many, who don't understand capitalism, cling to) don't hide it -- they invest it. They reinvest it into their businesses so it can grow bigger, stronger and give their customers better value for their money. They also invest it in other peoples' companies, resulting in these other entrepreneurs having money to expand their businesses; in the process, they take advantage of the miracle of compounding interest and as a result, make even more money.

What is the result of all this wealth in the hands of a single capitalist? In Bill Gates' case:

His company, Microsoft, and the extensions thereof have spawned an estimated 12,000 millionaires and four Billionaires. As of 2009, there were 93,000 employees receiving a very good income and excellent benefits for themselves and their families. Many other companies which do business with

Microsoft, et al, flourish and are able to employ untold numbers, and many start-ups and existing businesses have access to the capital they need. All these well-employed folks and their families have money to spend in their local communities, plus nationally and worldwide. As a result, there is plenty of money available to be given to any number of worthwhile causes and charities -- if these people wish to do so. The Gates Foundation, as of 2009, has an endowment of 33.5 billion, from which it has given a minimum of 1.5 billion to worthwhile causes annually

Now let's look at the other side of the coin. What if, after making his first million or two, Bill Gates had decided that having a couple of million dollars was as much as any one individual should have or needs to have and took his small fortune and closed up shop? What if he had decided to retire early and live off the interest on his first one or two-million-dollar earnings? Let's say that he decided to take $500,000 of his money to start a foundation to give grants to those in need. Giving away the interest on the half-million dollars each year, at an average of

10% interest, he could give away about $50,000 per year. In 20 years he would have given about a million dollars to worthwhile causes -- not bad. Of course, he wouldn't have created 12,000 millionaires who, if they gave just a miserly $1,000 each to charity, would be donating 12 million per year -- twelve times as much as Bill could give, under this early-retirement scenario, in 20 years!

Of course, we all know that Bill Gates didn't take his first piddly little two million and run. He did what many successful entrepreneurs do each year; he risked it all by reinvesting the money he had made back into the business with the hope and belief that he could make even more money and better serve his customers with ever better products and services that would make their lives better.

As a result of his keeping the vast bulk of his money through the early years, Bill Gates now has a foundation that can, with matching funds, give away billions of dollars here in the U.S. and around the world -- improving the quality of life for countless people. And this doesn't even include all the money given to charities by all the billionaires and millionaires resulting from his business acumen. Keep in mind that each little billion is a thousand million or a thousand times as much as Bill Gates could have given to those in need in 20 years if he had gone philanthropic too soon or too full bore.

We see that when a wealthy person such as Bill Gates keeps his money for himself, he is not really keeping it for himself, because this money is kept in circulation, growing the economy, creating countless jobs in innumerable businesses across the country and the world. Even when a rich person spends his money on food for parties, for a yacht or clothes, it helps to keep the party stores, yacht stores and clothing stores profitable so they can continue to employ their staffs. The truth is that the more rich people there are and the wealthier they are, the more there is for everyone else in that economy -- unless the wealthy one "puts it under his mattress."

Does this truth hold for one's health and fitness as well as for financial matters? Here is my question for you: When it comes to your health and fitness, is it better to take care of yourself first or your loved ones? If we allow ourselves to become rundown and sick because we ignore our own well-being while helping our loved ones, how much help will we be to them then? Making our own well-being our top priority creates more energy, strength, and vitality with which to care for those we love. When we have taken the time to make ourselves ultra-healthy and fit, we are also good role models and a positive example for all in our circle of influence -- including strangers we pass on the street.

Bill Gates kept the bulk of his money (invested it) for decades and we are all the beneficiaries of this choice. As a result of his taking care of business (taking care of himself and his "family" FIRST), he and those he helped to become rich can now help many, many more. We can learn from this model, whether we're talking about finances or health.

The Challenges and Failures He Faced

Bill Gates faced many challenges. One of the challenges is that when Microsoft first opened Bill Gates became very successful, but then when MITS found out Bill Gates age people all over the world stopped buying them for a while which led to financial problems which meant he did not get a lot of money but then came successful again later in life. Another challenge Bill Gates faced was that Bill Gates parents were not happy when he said that he wanted to drop out of college so he could start his company, but his parents said no. It took almost 1 year to convince Bill Gates parents to start the company in New Mexico. Bill Gates is very confident but have failed some things. One of the things that Bill Gates failed is that Bill Gates missed his offer of Giving the first BASIC that he was supposed to make but it took more than 5 weeks to make it when it was supposed to be made in 3 weeks. (second BASIC version.)

The First Failure that He Had

Before Bill Gates was successful in Microsoft, did he fail?

Yes of course.

Every great Entrepreneur has failed at one point, and will also continue to fail occasionally in their life. Failing at something is what makes Entrepreneurs as good as they are. Bill Gates is no exception.

In the early 1970s before Microsoft, Bill Gates and Paul Allen started a company called Traf-O-Data. It was a traffic analytical company that read data and created reports for engineers based on roads/highways. Allen quoted that between 1974–1980 Traf-O-Data had total losses of $3494 and they ended up shutting it down.

However, that failure is what gave Bill Gates the experience and understanding of the business that made Microsoft such as success. Had Bill Gates not experienced that failing prior, Microsoft would most likely never had been the success that it was. And this can be said for all Entrepreneurs. There is no a great Entrepreneur who doesn't have failings as well.

Failing is one of the best ways to learn and get to the top. Failing is what makes your next business opportunity have a higher chance of succeeding.

The Failure that Came After it and How He Dealt With it.

The man who started Microsoft and who was once worth 12 figures (not a typo) has revolutionized the tech industry through his business and changed the world through his foundation.

But, that doesn't mean it was easier for him when he started out than it is for anyone else. His first business failed, and while he was an excellent CEO, he made several big mistakes at Microsoft.

Bill Gates dealt with is the second failure which was an attempt at TV-style internet shows that ended up flopping. The weight of it all could have made him depressed, but instead he accepted those experiences as challenges and learned from them.

"Once you embrace unpleasant news not as a negative but as evidence of a need for change, you aren't defeated by it," Gates says in his book.

"You're learning from it. It's all in how you approach failures."

Like so many business "failure" stories, this one is more a story about sewing seeds of success. See, Traf-O-Data forced Gates and Allen to learn programming skills that would be critical for building Microsoft a few years later. In a 1995 article with Fortune Magazine, Paul Allen acknowledged:

"Even though Traf-O-Data wasn't a roaring success, it was seminal in preparing us to make Microsoft's first product a couple of years later."

There are so many stories of successful business people who failed early in their careers for one, simple reason: success is borne out of failure. All the best businesspeople - Gates, Jobs, Musk, etc. - learned to use big failures to thrust themselves forward towards enormous successes!

8.2 The Rise and Rise of Bill Gates

As the co-founder and chairman of the mammoth Microsoft Corporation, Bill Gates is the moving force behind a company that has been regarded as "The Most Innovative Company Operating in the U.S." (1993, Forbes magazines). Microsoft introduced several revolutionary technological advancements in the computer industry that made the company the first truly dominant player among home computer operating systems. Microsoft also created the most widely used operating system in the world, Microsoft Windows.

Gates is widely regarded as the brains behind the Microsoft Corporation, primarily responsible for product strategy from the time the company was founded in 1975 until 2006. Among his key contributions are extensively broadening the company's product lines and vigorously defending Microsoft's dominant position in its key areas of operation. And while some of his decisions have led to antitrust litigation over Microsoft's business practices, his reputation as one of the most popular and respected entrepreneurs of the personal computer revolution remains intact. His fame actually surpasses the realm of computers and business and extends into mainstream society. For instance, in a 2006 list compiled by New Statesman magazine, Gates was voted eighth in the "Heroes of Our Time" category.

In June 2006, Gates announced that he will be handing the reins of Microsoft's day-to-day operations to someone else by July 2008 to concentrate on the philanthropic work of the Bill and Melinda Gates Foundation, although he will continue to serve as the company's chairman and as an advisor on special projects. Plans are already afoot to transfer Gates' role as Chief Software Architect of Microsoft to Ray Ozzie, the former head honcho of the Groove company which Microsoft purchased in 2005.

Gates has donated several millions of dollars to various charitable groups and scientific research studies. By some estimates, Gates has contributed over half his fortune to charity. Even if such were the case, he can easily afford it. Recently, the prestigious Forbes magazine named Gates as the world's richest person for the 12th straight year, with a 2006 net worth of $50 billion. Incidentally, he actually became the world's first "centibillionaire" in 1999 when his net worth surpassed the 100 billion mark briefly.

How Did Bill Gates Became So Rich?

People all across the world ask themselves the same question whenever they hear his name; how did Bill Gates become so rich? It's a valid question for any logical person to ask considering Mr. Gates has perennially been listed as one of the richest people in the world for the last 16 years. What magic does he possess that puts him in such an exclusive class of people? Let's look at the 10 primary reasons to answer that question:

1.   Bill Gates is passionate about his work; he absolutely loves what he does and doesn't view his business as a chore. When you love what you do you are able to stay strong when times get tough and also want to get better at what you do. Working is a way of life for Bill Gates.

2.   He is a voracious learner. He has a strong hold on a wide variety of subjects and this feeds his impetus to stay curious with his work, as well as providing him with

a greater understanding of what he does. He understands that the day his curiosity is gone is the same day his wealth is gone too.

3.   He doesn't do it for the money. Yes, money is the medium through which one keeps score in their business and life, but attachment to it will never bring you the results you desire. Bill Gates instead puts his focus on the process of his work, rather than the money, trying to create the absolute best business that he is capable of creating. When you remove the concern for money and instead focus on the task at hand you will perform your best and ironically be in a better position to earn the most money for yourself. Don't be in it for the money.

4.   He is a technician. By learning all the technical aspects of his business from the ground up he completely understood his business inside out. He commands respect from all his employees because he knows their jobs better than they do. There is nothing he can't do within his business.

5.   Bill Gates learns from the mistakes of other businesses and people and makes

certain that the same will not happen with his company. He investigates all companies and industries to see where they fell short and has trained his business to look for the same pitfalls.

6.   He looks for people as smart as he is that have the ability to think independently and solve problems. He wants those that think just like he does.

7.   His mastery of logic and strategy has shaped a philosophy around his business decisions that allows him to outsmart all of his competitors.

8.   When one project is doing well he is somewhere making another one happen. He has never been complacent with his present circumstance and doesn't rely on it to keep bringing him success. It is about being in perpetual motion and always looking for new avenues of income in case one goes dry.

9.   He sacrificed a high-paying salary for more stock options in the early days of Microsoft. He bet on the strength of his company in doing this, reinvesting his personal money right back into the

company. He focused on how well the company performed and his equity stake in it.

10.   He has an open mind. Nathan Myhrvold, one of his top guys at Microsoft, has stated how open Mr. Gates is with problem-solving within the company. He believes that a group problem-solving atmosphere is more productive than having one or two people constantly coming up with all the answers. He knows that no person, no matter how smart they may be, has all the answers.

9.2The 5 Wealth Secrets That Made Bill Gates Very Rich and Successful

Bill Gates is easily one of the richest homo sapiens walking on planet earth. How did he make it? This chapter gives you the 5 Wealth Secrets that made Bill very rich and successful; and which you can adopt, adapt or modify to become rich and successful too. Please read on!

1.   He started early.

Born in 1955, Bill's first contact with the computer was in 1968, at the tender age of 13. At a very young age, he became interested in computer software and programming and used his school's computer to practice because computers were still very expensive to own. His interest and enthusiasm for programming were uncommon. It was passionate.

2.   He was Passionate and Committed.

Bill was very passionate about computer software and programming. Thus, as a student at Lakeside Prep School, he spent his days and nights designing and writing computer programs. Accordingly, this took a heavy toll on his academic performance, as classes were skipped and homework left undone.

At the Computer Centre Corporation, Bill and his friends crashed the system several times and even sabotaged the security system, all in their passionate uest to acquire new computer skills. But when they hacked into and altered the algorithm that recorded computer usage time, they were promptly banned for several weeks!

3.   He quickly became his own Boss.

Bill Gates started his university education at Harvard in 1973, but had to drop out in 1975 to take care of Business: with his friend Paul Allen, he set up Microsoft Corporation in 1975.

Obviously, he dropped out of Harvard, not for lack of capacity or capability for higher education, but because his heart was not in his studies. Bill was so committed to his dream that he refused to be distracted even by the allure of formal education at the prestigious Harvard University!

4.   He added great value and was greatly rewarded.

While still at school, Bill and three of his colleague's set up a team called the Lakeside Programmers, on which platform they struck a deal with Computer Centre Corporation. The team reviewed computer programs to identified bugs and other problems. For this, they were allowed unlimited computer usage time at the Centre. Hear him: "It was when we got free time at the Computer Centre that we really got into computers"

Next, the Lakeside Programmers were hired by Information Science Incorporated to create a payroll program. For this, they again got free computer time as well as royalties from sales of the software.

And for Traf-O-Data, Bill and his friend Allen created a software that helps measure traffic flow. This earned them about $20,000.

Under Microsoft Corporation, Bill gave the world the computer operating system software called WINDOWS. Put conservatively, WINDOWS runs in over sixty percent of all computers on planet earth! Bill gave the world great products and services and was greatly rewarded.

5.   He generously gave back to Humanity

Through his published books, Bill continues to increase Knowledge and bless the World by sharing his Wisdom and Ideas; through his Products and Services, he continues to add Value to our lives; and through the Bill and Melinda Gates Foundation, he continues to give his Money away to bless and uplift Humanity. What a great way to serve God and Man; and what else is the Purpose of Life, after all?

Bill Gates will be remembered, not for what he took out of the world for himself, but for what he gave to the world of himself. And for being such a beautiful inspiration to our Youths.

5 Lessons Bill Gates Could Teach You

Smart Internet marketers know that buying master resale rights is a shortcut to getting products on the market. But did you know that Bill Gates and the Microsoft empire were built from purchasing master resale rights?

That's right - Bill Gates bought the rights to DOS, the operating system that began the Microsoft empire.

There are 5 important lessons Bill Gates could teach you about master resale rights.

1.   Find a hungry market with a burning need and fill it

Bill Gates read about the Altair 8800 computer in Popular Science in 1975.

Realizing Altair needed a simple programming language to make the computer popular, Gates sold a version of BASIC to Altair before it was even written. Then Gates worked night and day with Paul Allen and Monte Davidoff to develop it. Microsoft was born.

In 1980, IBM created the desktop PC - but they didn't have an operating system. Gates saw a burning need waiting to be filled, and learned a new lesson:

2. You don't have to create a product to fill a need if you can buy the master resale rights instead.

IBM approached Bill Gates to create an operating system for the PC. Gates initially recommended they contact Digital Research to purchase their CP/M operating system. But those negotiations failed, and IBM came back to Bill Gates.

Gates learned that Tim Paterson of Seattle Computer Products had developed a clone of CP/M called QDOS. Microsoft bought the rights for just $56,000.

Of course, you don't have to invest $56,000 to get rights worth selling. Often you can buy master resale rights for $100, $50, even $10 or $20. You can even join resale rights membership sites and get thousands of dollars worth of products for a small monthly fee. Sometimes you can even find master resale rights products for free!

Why so cheap? Sometimes the products aren't very good, but often they're great products that weren't marketed well. Not seeing the opportunity, people sell their work for almost nothing.

Smart marketers know that sometimes you can just rename a product or change the marketing and have a hit. This is where Bill Gates could teach us the third lesson:

3.   Repackage or rebrand, change the marketing approach, and build your own brand.

QDOS stood for "Quick and Dirty Operating System." IBM might have bought it even with a name like that, but being a savvy marketer, Gates decided to rebrand it. He dubbed it "PC-DOS," for "PC Disk Operating System." He targeted it squarely at IBM - and they bought it, big time.

When PC clones hit the market, Gates saw another hungry market with a burning need. Microsoft quickly rebranded DOS, dubbing it "MS-DOS" for "Microsoft Disk Operating System," thus building the Microsoft brand at the same time. The rest is history.

Resale rights products are often widely available. If you do the same thing as everyone else, why should someone buy the product from you? But if you take the time to repackage or rebrand the resale rights where permitted, you will have a unique product you can market to a hungry audience with a burning need. Because the next lesson we can learn from Bill Gates is:

4.   Just because someone else didn't become a billionaire with the master resale rights for a product doesn't mean you can't. Use your brain and figure out how to do things better.

Success in any business is often as dependent on intelligence, motivation, and marketing as it is on the product itself.

Others created the BASIC programming language, but Bill Gates repackaged it and sold it to Altair. Digital Research had a perfect operating system for the PC, but they missed out. Tim Paterson created the DOS operating system that would run every PC in the world. But he sold it to Microsoft for $56,000. Bill Gates is now worth an estimated $51 billion. Forbes magazine says he is the richest man in the world.

Realizing he had a hungry market with a burning need, Gates saw opportunities that others missed, took products that were relative failures, and built a multi-billion dollar empire.

Not everyone is Bill Gates, but don't you think we all have opportunities that we either take or miss? And don't you think we sometimes settle for less than we could have?

That brings us to the final lesson that Bill Gates could teach you about master resale rights:

5.   Don't sell your life for almost anything.

Bill Gates took opportunities that others had and did something with them. Do you think Bill Gates would ever sell the master resale rights to all of the Microsoft products for $10?

Of course not! Yet you will often see people selling master resale rights to great products for less than you'd spend for dinner! They don't realize they are selling their life for almost nothing.

You can't go far on the Internet without someone promising you that you can make a million dollars by selling their product. Do you realize how many $10 products you would have to sell every day to make a million dollars a year? 274! Each and every day, 365 days a year. Wouldn't it be easier to sell 27.4 copies of a product every day for $100 each? Or a $30 monthly membership to a site 8 times a day?

You're not going to see Microsoft selling the next version of Windows for $10 each, and you shouldn't sell yourself short either.

Don't drop your price. Build your marketing skills instead. Find a hungry market with a burning need. Fill it by creating your own repackaged, rebranded product from other people's master resale rights products. Use your brain and figure out how to do it

133

better. Don't sell your life for anything. Charge a higher price and make it worth it to people. Fulfill their need and you'll have no shortage of business.

10.2 Ways to Be More Like Bill Gates

1.   Never Stop Learning

There is a lot of value attached to being exposed to various experiences from an early age. When Bill Gates was in the ninth grade his school bought an early personal computer making Gates completely enthralled with the devices.

Gates was allowed to leave his mathematics class to learn programming. The first program he ever created was a Tic-Tac-Toe game. He never looked back. In college, Gates made it a habit of sitting in on classes for which he had never even signed up. Gates continued this thirst for knowledge to this day.

2.   Take on a Big Enough Mission

In some ways, this should be the first item on the list, as truly successful people first choose endeavors worthy of their time.

In Gates's case, fast-forward to the 2000s, after he transitioned out of Microsoft and became a full-time philanthropist. Using the examples of John Rockefeller and Andrew Carnegie (and the mentorship of Warren Buffett), Gates and his wife, Melinda Gates, are among America's most generous philanthropists, focusing on "big problems" that they believe governments around the world are incapable of solving.

3.   Risk-Taking

Bill Gates risked his future when he dropped out of Harvard when only 20 years old, to co-found the software company, Microsoft.

From Bill Gates' book, "Businessat the Speed of Thought: Using a Digital Nervous System", Bill describes his risk-taking as "to win big, sometimes you have to take big risks. Big bets mean big failures as well as successes. Today, looking back, it's easy to believe that Microsoft's current success was inevitable. But at the time we made our big bets, including starting the company as the first personal computer software firm, most people thought we would fail."

4.   Business is a Money Game with few Rules and a lot of Risks

What are the things you are most afraid of doing that has the potential to grow your business the most or put you on the most direct path to where you want to be? One way to overcome the fear of taking risks is simply through exposure.

To break out of your comfort zone, and start taking more risks with your business, spend more time with people who encourage you, not the ones who think you will fail.

5.   Learn From Your Mistakes

Learning from one's mistakes is one of the biggest factors in maturity and growth. Bad decisions and their aftermaths furnish us with the most important lessons we can ever learn. Experience cannot be your teacher unless you are willing to heed the lessons.

Bill Gates once related that the success of Microsoft was in part due to the success of his leadership team in recognizing mistakes;

mistakes that could prove costly in the future. Gates wasn't afraid of changing course once a decision showed itself as being ill-advised. Unfortunately, for far too many people, it takes a lot of mistakes to learn a single lesson. Learning from our mistakes helps us to develop wisdom and discernment.

6.   Be the Guy who Predicts the Future

Obviously easier said than done, but Gates saw the future first at several key moments. One of them--and this is a classic story-- came in 1980, when he negotiated a deal to license the DOS operating system to IBM for a low $50,000, but had the foresight not transfer the copyright. As a result, Microsoft was able to license the OS to other vendors who cloned IBM's machine, thus making a much bigger and more profitable market for his company.

More chillingly: Gates has said recently he's concerned about the threats of super-intelligent machines on humanity. Let's hope he's not seeing this prediction as clearly.

7.   Seek Forgiveness, Not Permission

Too many people fail to succeed because they hold themselves back. Whether it was youthful folly or instinct, Gates didn't fall into this category.

As an early example--that computer in eighth grade? When the school's funds eventually ran out, Gates (with his friend Paul Allen and other students) exploited bugs to obtain free computer time. When they were caught, he and the others traded their bug-finding ability for more free computer time.

10.3Inspiring Bill Gates Quotes on How to Succeed in Life

One of the world's top philanthropists, Bill Gates is as generous and giving as he is wealthy and successful. Gates is investing a big part of his fortune in making the world a better place for the poor. He saved over 5 million lives by bringing vaccines and improving children healthcare; throughout his life, he donated half of his current worth; he invested in a foundation that supports much health, social and education developments, and the list goes on.

Here's the cold, hard, honest truth. You have to be a taker before you can be a giver, otherwise, you have nothing to give. There is no virtue in remaining small so as not to appear greedy. Bill Gates knew this, and he built himself up into someone truly capable of making a difference in the world. If you are sitting around complaining about how much money he has, what difference are you making in people's lives?

Meanwhile Bill Gates is contributing to AIDS research, reducing world hunger, and all in all, being an outstanding citizen of the world. If you resent the success of others, you will only deprive yourself. If your belief is that successful, rich people are greedy and evil and selfish, and you feel that you are a good person, then how will you ever be able to become wealthy and still feel that you are a good person?

The next time you notice yourself have negative feelings towards someone who is more successful than you (and this can be anyone from Donald Trump to your next door neighbor), why not stop as ask yourself why?. The Limelight is about living life creatively and finding inspiration to do so.

Success didn't make Gates selfish and arrogant, but wise, so here are 5 Bill Gates ⵁuotes to help you succeed and never forget being kind to others.

1.   Don't compare yourself with anyone in this world. If you do so, you are insulting yourself.

2.   We make the future sustainable when we invest in the poor, not when we insist on their suffering.

3.   Discrimination has a lot of layers that make it tough for minorities to get a leg up.

4.   If you think your teacher is tough, wait 'til you get a boss. He doesn't have tenure.

5.   Be nice to nerds. Chances are you'll end up working for one.

10.4 Gates of success

Undoubtedly, Bill Gates has been a phenomenon. He has been featured in the Forbes 400 list of the wealthiest people in the world for 15 years in a row between 1993 and 2007. He has occupied the numero uno position in the list of richest people from 1995 to 2007. For a brief period in 1999, his net worth went past $100 billion, and the new term "centibillionaire" was coined.

Success of Microsoft

Bill Gates' key creation is Microsoft, a company with sales of $51 billion as of June 2007 with 78,000 employees across 105 countries. Almost 90% of the estimated 1 billion computers (desktop and laptop) in the world are run on Microsoft's Windows and Office. The company has products across the layers network, operating system, database, middleware, application software. There are technologies that power handheld devices and smartphones, software services, hardware and entertainment devices like Tablet PC, Xbox and IPTV technology. The launch of Windows on November 20, 1985, brought Microsoft into the mainstream system of software. Its Windows 95 launch on August 25 saw a marketing blitzkrieg worth $1 billion on the day of the launch.

Awards

In addition to being one of the richest and most successful businessmen in the history of the world, Bill Gates has also received numerous awards for philanthropic work. Time magazine named Gates one of the most influential people of the 20th century. The magazine also named Gates and his wife Melinda, along with rock band U2's lead singer, Bono, as the 2005 Persons of the Year.

Gates holds several honorary doctorates from universities throughout the world. He was knighted as an honorary Knight Commander of the Order of the British Empire bestowed by Queen Elizabeth II in 2005.

In 2006, Gates and his wife were awarded the Order of the Aztec Eagle by the Mexican government for their philanthropic work throughout the world in the areas of health and education. In 2016, Gates and his wife Melinda were recognized for their philanthropic work when they were named recipients of the Presidential Medal of Freedom by President Barack Obama.

In early 2018, Gates achieved another distinction with the announcement he would guest star on an episode of The Big Bang Theory. The sitcom's honor roll of guest stars includes Leonard Nimoy and George Takei of Star Trek fame, entrepreneur Elon Musk and scientists Stephen Hawking and Bill Nye.

Chapter 11: Bill Gates Inventions- Top-Greatest Hits And Misses

Internet Explorer (IE)

Introduced 1995

It's really easy to simply remember "Internet Exploder" as the standards-breaking, web-forking, buggy, monopoly-causing app that helped shape Bill's old image as the evilest baron of all technology companies. But it's also the app that led to the creation Ajax-based web apps through the XMLHttpRe?uest spec, and the kludgey early popularization of CSS. Love it or hate it, IE's gotten more people on the web over the years than any browser, and that's definitely got to count for something.

Media Center

Introduced 2002

Despite TiVo's DVR dominance and competitors that came and went over the years, Media Center has always been an underrated standout product. Even Bill admits that the company's long struggled with usability, but Media Center is a beacon of hope not only for 10-foot UIs everywhere, but also for the company's ability to create powerful, advanced, user-friendly products. Between its online integration, extensible plugin architecture, ability to stream shows to nodes around the house, and now CableCARD support, the only real downside to Media Center is the fact that you still need a full-blown PC to run it.

MS-DOS

Introduced 1981, discontinued 2000

It was arcane and nigh-unusable to mere mortals -- but the early cash-cow was one of Bill's most strategic moves, and helped Microsoft define the concept of software licensing. It also helped launched Mossberg's career as crusader of user-friendly technology. But most importantly, MS-DOS was still the OS an entire generation grew up learning, so del criticism.* for a second because our autoexec.bat and config.sys were so very well crafted, and extensively tweaking Memmaker for a few extra KB of usable RAM definitely ranks amongst our top most formative geek moments.

Office

Introduced 1989 (on Mac), 1990 (on PC)

Word, Excel and PowerPoint certainly did well enough on their own, but when Microsoft combined 'em into the tidy (and pricey) package that is Office -- first on the Mac in 1989, interestingly -- it had a selling point that would prove irresistible to many a productivity-obsessed middle manager even today. The addition of Outlook and it's support for the (for some) nigh-indispensable Exchange only further solidified its foothold in the corporate computing world, and that's where Bill knew the real money was. That's certainly not to say that it hasn't been without its share of problems and annoyances, though -- we're looking at you, Clippy.

Peripherals

Introduced 1982

Microsoft has always been a software company first, but it's been cranking out high-quality peripherals for over 25 years -- long before the Xbox and Zune were even a twinkle in Bill's eye. Not only that, but it's been a reliable innovator in the field, with a string of devices that were first, early, or just simply popularized technologies like the wheel mouse, force-feedback joysticks and controllers, the modern optical mouse, and the ergo-keyboard. The division has gone through some bumpy times -- the SideWinder line was killed off for a while there, and there've been some questionable designs along the way -- but it's been riding high as of late, and it doesn't show any signs of slowing down soon.

Windows 3.1 / NT 3.5

Introduced 1992 and 1994

It took a few versions to come into its own, but by the time Windows hit 3.1, Microsoft finally had a product that was able to pull PC users away from the command line (for some of the time, at least) and give them a real taste of things to come. Windows NT may not have had quite the same appeal with the average consumer, but it did bring the operating system into the 32-bit world and pave the way for enterprise desktop computing as we know it today. (Plus, it had the NT file system (NTFS), which to this day continues to carry on the legacy in its own little way.) We really wish they'd made a sequel to the Pirates of Silicon Valley, because we'd love to have seen the dramatization of Bill overseeing the first popularized versions of Windows -- especially '95, which came out just a couple of years later.

Windows 2000 and XP

Introduced 2000

When thinking of Microsoft and the new millennium, few people are able to keep the crinkles out of their nose. Thankfully, Windows ME wasn't the only thing that arrived in late Y2K, as Windows 2000 rushed in to rock the socks off of suits everywhere. The whole Win2K thing went over so well that Gates and company decided to base its next consumer OS, XP, off of it. Some may argue that the resulting product still stands as the last great OS to ship out of Redmond.

Windows CE / Mobile

Introduced 1996

As two of the most ubiԀuitous projects to come out from under Bill's command, both Windows CE and Windows Mobile are almost impossible to avoid when it comes to handhelds or phones. What began as a mishmash of small components has grown into the adaptable -- though sometimes maddening -- mobile OS that resides on just about every kind of device you can think of.

Really, we mean every kind of device, from PMPs to enterprise-level stock-keeping systems. The slimmed down and restructured micro-Windows is at the very least one of the more flexible offerings the company has ever produced. Say what you will about its usability, there's no denying the massive impact it's had on portability and convergence.

Xbox and Xbox 360

Introduced 2001 and 2005

Back in 1999, Bill was all about multimedia convergence, and he said that a new gaming / multimedia device would be Microsoft's trojan horse into the world's living rooms with something coined the "DirectX-box." In 2001, the original Xbox entered gaming territory dominated by Sony's PlayStation with Nintendo's N64. But the clunky machine brought with it the first easy to use multiplayer console service, Xbox Live, as well as a developer-centric model that helped turn the tables. Of course, things look quite a bit different today: the Xbox

360 leads the former market leader's PlayStation 3 in spend and attach rate, and with the relative success of media and content sales on Xbox Live, it seems Bill's dream of dominating the living room wasn't just a pipe-dream after all.

Visual Basic

Introduced 1991, discontinued 1998

It's hard to underestimate the impact of Visual Basic. While the average user might have never heard of the original VB that Microsoft released way back when, the simplicity of the language and its graphical toolset made just about any power user a potential app developer, powering the flood of third party application development Microsoft operating systems enjoyed throughout the 90's. Sadly, Visual Basic met its demise at the hands of more modern languages and toolsets, but with a legacy of making programming accessible to the masses, its place in the history books and in Bill's pocketbook is undoubtedly secure.

Misses

Auto PC

Introduced 1998, discontinued 2001

Riding high on its previously-introduced sister products -- the Handheld PC and Palm PC platforms, now dead and transformed into Windows Mobile, respectively -- Microsoft's Auto PC initiative was promised to herald a revolution for in-car entertainment and productivity. There's no question it was well ahead of its time; in fact, many of the features debuted in Auto PC have gone on to become standard fare in today's cars. Problem was when it launched your ride was already pimped with a mere CD player. In-car navigation, voice recognition, and MP3 support were still the stuff of science fiction in those dark days (particularly at the four-digit asking price), and the whole thing was doomed to a geeky, spendy niche. Though products were initially expected from several manufacturers, Clarion ended up being the only one to actually produce a head unit.

*The Auto PC lived on in spirit as Clarion's Joyride, but Microsoft's heart was no longer in the project and Clarion had switched to a generic Windows CE-based core to build the product.

Microsoft Bob

Introduced 1995, discontinued 1996

Poor Bob. No one ever gave him a chance. Maybe it had to do with the fact that he was really annoying. And as it turns out, Bill was dating Melinda French, Bob's program manager. Which isn't to say there was any nepotism involved -- Bob suffered an early death in 1996 due to general hatred for the little bastard. Bill offered this to a column in January 1997, "Unfortunately, [Bob] demanded more performance than typical computer hardware could deliver at the time and there wasn't an ade◻uately large market. Bob died." Thankfully, Billinda's blossoming relationship lived on. Oh, did you hear? They're like the world's greatest philanthropists now.

Cairo

Introduced 1991 (but never released)

Ask folks to pick one word to describe Microsoft's technology roadmap in the 1990s and you'll commonly get "Cairo" in response. Announced before Windows NT 3.1 was even released, Cairo was occasionally an operating system, occasionally a collection of new technologies -- it depended entirely upon who and when you asked -- but at its core, it was intended to guide Microsoft on the path beyond the architecture introduced by NT. After throwing countless dollars and man-hours at the ambitious project, Cairo was ultimately canned (though mentions of the storied buzzword continued even into this decade). Although Windows 2000 eventually became NT's heir apparent, the fruits of Microsoft's labor weren't entirely for naught, as various Cairo features found themselves implanted into various versions of Windows throughout the years. Even the WinFS file system can trace its roots back to the project -- fitting, because it too has become such an albatross.

MSN Music and URGE

Introduced 2004 and 2006, both fully discontinued 2008

When MSN Music -- Microsoft's effort to build its own PlaysForSure-based subscription music based store -- imploded, headstrong Bill did what he usually does: rebrand and launch again. When he got up at CES 2006 and announced MSN Music would become URGE with MTV, we were all a little skeptical -- after all, the problem wasn't really the service, it was the overbearing DRM and the fact that consumers simply weren't ready for subscription music. Of course, eventually URGE died as well, and MTV shunted customers to Rhapsody America; naturally, Microsoft had a third PlaysForSure-based store waiting in the wings with Zune, which doesn't appear to be going anywhere any time soon.

Origami / UMPC

Introduced 2006

UMPCs... what can we say? Sure, Scoble liked them, but even from day one we never saw the market potential. Fueled by an early and too-successful hype-generating viral campaign of Microsoft's own making, there was no way that these first generation Origami devices would achieve their promise. Overpriced, underpowered, desktop OS-laden (with Microsoft's Touch Pack add-on), and poor battery life all helped ensure drown UMPCs in the wave of "ultramobile lifestyle PC"-hysteria they rode to market. And as UMPCs begin to fade, the shrinking niche between smartphones and laptops can look forward to the sweet release of MIDs -- though that's already been two years... and counting.

OS/2

Dates: introduced 1987, discontinued 2006

What began as a collaboration between Microsoft and then-partner IBM blossomed into what looked like -- for a time at least -- the logical successor to the DOS / Windows empire. The advanced OS showed early signs of greatness with it's incorporation of the HPFS file system, improved networking capabilities, and a sophisticated UI. But cracks in the relationship between the two powerhouse corporations would ultimately lead to its downfall. With Windows 3 a sudden success, IBM's reluctance to go hardware neutral, and Microsoft's increasing displeasure with code which it called "bloated" (ahem!), the project was eventually swept aside by Gates and the gang to make way for what would become the omnipresent operating system you know and love and/or hate today.

SPOT watches and MSN Direct

Introduced 2004, discontinued 2008

When the concept of an information-enabled watch that automagically received content over unused FM radio subcarriers was first conjured up by Microsoft in the early part of the decade, it seemed like a fabulous idea. So much so, in fact, Bill personally took the project under his wing. But by the time it had launched, it was already doomed by a perfect storm of problems: the devices were uglier than sin and comically oversized, the bizarre ad campaign featured frighteningly hairy cartoon arms, and -- as the mobile web was just starting to pick up steam at that time -- virtually anyone who would've been interested in that kind of product had already discovered ways to get the same information from their phone. The underlying data network Microsoft built out to support the watches, MSN Direct, lives on to this day and sees plenty of use in Garmin's nüvi line, but will it ever be used to beam weather, news, and MSFT stock reports to wrists other than Bill's? Not bloody likely.

Windows Activation

Introduced 2001

Depending on who you talk to, Windows Product Activation is a serious privacy violation, a headache, minimal protection against piracy, or all of the above. Lucky for us, Microsoft is finally seeing (some of) the folly of its overbearing ways and has gone with a more permissive nagware method with Vista SP1. This as opposed to the regular method of routinely locking users out of their systems, which, would not you know it, tended to hurt legitimate users more than pirates. Perhaps the best example of Windows Activation's legacy was the great WGA outage of 2007, which left 12,000 systems out in the cold due to few downed servers at Microsoft. It didn't take long for the servers to bounce back, but any shred of reputation the service had at that point went out the window with the uptime.

Windows ME

Introduced September 2000

It's not exactly clear what the point of Windows Millennium Edition was -- our guess is that Microsoft needed to keep up with that year-based product naming scheme it had going at the time, and cranked out this half-baked update to '98 in order to capitalize on the turn-of-the-millennium frenzy. Unlike the NT-based Windows 2000 released at the same time, Windows ME retained its MS-DOS-based core while managing to somehow get even more slow and unstable than its predecessors 95 and 98. And to add insult to injury, it restricted access to shell mode, rendering many MS-DOS apps incompatible. Thankfully, Windows ME was only inflicted upon consumers for little over a year; it was replaced by indomitable Windows XP in 2001.

Windows Vista

Introduced 2007

Vista doesn't suck. Let's just get that off our chests. In fact, it's a ⬚uite capable, secure and sexy OS when you get right down to it. Unfortunately, its problems just loomed too large for many folks to overlook. A multitude of delays and a rapidly diminishing feature list soured people right out of the gate, and once the dust settled people just weren't happy with the minor improvements they were getting in exchange for their hard-earned monies and fairly mandatory RAM upgrades. Mix that in with the standard driver incompatibilities of any Microsoft OS upgrade, and you've got a whole bunch of disgruntled downgraders on your hands -- and plenty of bad press to fill in any remaining gaps. Sadly, improvements to Media Center, aesthetics and even that ⬚uirky little sidebar got overlooked in the process. Microsoft's already scrambling to get Windows 7 together to capture the multitude of users that have decided to skip Vista altogether, let's just hope it's not too late.

Chapter 12: Education And Marriage

William Henry Gates III was born in Seattle, Washington on October 28th, 1955. Bills father Bill Gates Jr. worked for a Seattle law firm and Bills mother Mary, taught school until they started their family. Bills parents were married in 1951 and two years later gave birth to their first child, Bills older sister, Kristanne. Two years after that Bill was born and in 1964 the third and final Gates was born, her name is Libby. As a child Bill enjoyed rocking back and forth, today he still has a habit of rocking when he is thinking about something. Bill was very bored at school and his parents knew it so they were always trying to feed him more information to keep him busy. Bills parents finally decided to put him in a private school where he would be challenged more. The Lakeside private school had just bought a new computer when Bill arrived and he was immediately hooked. Within a week he had surpassed the knowledge of the computer teacher at Lakeside. Learning the BASIC programming language was a breeze for Bill and he was soon writing his own programs. Bills love for computers and math led him to a new place around his neighborhood that was renting computer time. He got an arrangement with the owners that he would get free computer time if he found things that would make the computer crash. During this time Bill met Paul Allen his business partner for the rest of his life. Together they started a small company called Traf-O-Data, they sold a small computer outfitted with their program that could count traffic for the city. This company wasn't a big success but it did earn the two boys some money as well as good business skills. Bill also wrote a schedule program for his school which he modified a bit to put little Bill Gates in a class full of the prettiest girls in the school. Bill was deemed by his peers and his teachers as the smartest kid on campus. Upon graduating from Lakeside Bill enrolled in Harvard University in 1973, one of the best universities in the country. Bill was also bored here so he spent most of his time programming, playing poker and seeing how little work he could do and still get A's. He told his teachers that he would be a millionaire by the time he was 30, this was one of the few times he underestimated himself, Bill was a billionaire when he was 31. One of Bills teachers was quoted saying "He was a helluva good programmer, but he's an obnoxious human being." The intense lifestyle Bill lived during his first year in Harvard made him ill for most of the summer of 1974. Bill soon left Harvard for business opportunities in programming which turned him into a multi-billionaire. Later he met Melinda French who he married and they now have a little daughter named Jennifer. It's very interesting that even with all that money Bill drives himself to work in an average family car and he even flies coach. A very interesting man and a very interesting childhood.

How he met melinda,his wife

In summer 1986, freshly graduated from Duke University with a degree in computer science and economics, Melinda Ann French was working as an intern for IBM. She told a recruiter she had one more interview – with a new company called Microsoft. The recruiter was keen. "If you get a job offer from them," she said, "take it because the chance for advancement there is terrific."

Indeed. Six-and-a-half years later, Melinda Ann had advanced through the company, from software marketing tyro to general manager of information products such as Expedia and Encarta; more significantly, she had advanced to a senior role in the heart of the chief executive, Bill Gates, soon to become the world's richest man. Today, she is one half of the world's top charity foundation, with personal jurisdiction over the spending of $80bn (£40bn). Clever, raven-haired, strong-featured and tough as nails, she brings eᵩual amounts of compassion, common sense and business nous to the small matter of alleviating world sickness and poverty.

Born in 1964, she grew up in Dallas, Texas, the daughter of Ray French, an engineer and house-rentals agent. At school, Melinda was earnest, driven and goal-orientated. Her introduction to the cyber-world came at 14 when her father brought home an Apple II, one of the first consumer computers available. She was soon playing computer games, and learning the Basic programming language.

It has always amused Bill Gates that his wife is better educated than him – he is America's most famous college drop-out. They met in 1987, four months into her job at Microsoft, when they sat next to each other at an Expo trade-fair dinner in New York. "He was funnier than I expected him to be," she reported, neutrally. Months went by before, meeting her in the Microsoft car park, he asked her out – in two weeks' time. She said, "ask me nearer the time." He had to explain to her the ceaseless daily flood of meetings.

Whatever first attracted Ms French to Bill Gates, he was struck by her forthrightness and independence. It was she who first spurred him into impulses of charity. After their engagement in 1993, during Melinda's "wedding shower", her mother Mary, suffering from breast cancer, read her an admonitory letter whose gist was, "from those to whom much is given, much is expected". Mary died months later, but her advice provoked the William H Gates Foundation. Run by Bill's father, its aim was to put laptops in every classroom. Then the couple decided that the most pressing issue in the US was reforming the education system.

Then, after their wedding in Hawaii (on New Year's Day 1994) Melinda read in The New York Times about the millions of children in developing countries dying of malaria and TB. She made world poverty their priority concern.

Melinda now spends 30 hours a week on foundation work, as she and Bill assess the charity presentations that flood in. Of the 6,000 re?uests the foundation receives each year, they read only the ones asking for $40m or more. "We go down the chart of the greatest ine?uities, and give where we can effect the greatest change," she told Forbes magazine, in a tone that suggests she doesn't regard it as rocket science. The foundation also links up with other charities and companies like Glaxo on more ambitious projects – like the Global Alliance for Vaccines and Immunisations, which kicked off with donations of $1.5m from each of 17 governments.

It's hard to keep sight of the woman behind the world's top charity: the high-achieving schoolgirl who loved complicated jigsaws and once scaled the 14,000ft Mount Rainier with ropes and crampons; the mother of three; and the devout Catholic who visited Calcutta to talk to Aids sufferers in Mother Teresa's Home for the Dying. But it's clear that the Foundation needs her clarity and good sense. Time magazine, when it put Bill Gates and Bono on the cover as "Person[s] of the Year," included Melinda Gates because she is the heart, as well as the brains, of the organisation. "Lots of people like Bill — and I include myself — are enraged," said Bono, "and we sweep ourselves into a fury at the wanton loss of lives. We need a much slower pulse to help us to be rational. Melinda is that pulse."

BILL GATES AND STEVE JOBS RELATIONSHIP

Looking back at Steve Jobs' tenure at Apple, it's impossible to separate the role Microsoft and Bill Gates played. The companies helped pioneer the industry and define an era. The two CEOs partnered at various times, competed all the time, and challenged one another in ways that helped shape the landscape of technology. It's a complex relationship — which you can witness in this amusing video compilation of Steve Jobs best ⍰uotes about Microsoft.

Let's look a little deeper into the history of this two great men.

Friends (1981 to 1983)

During the development of the Macintosh in the early 80s, Microsoft was an important ally. Apple needed groundbreaking software for it's upcoming platform and Microsoft was one of the few companies developing for it. It was a crucial phase for Apple.

The strength of their relationship could be witnessed at an Internal Apple Event in Hawai where Steve Jobs introduced the Macintosh to a few Apple VIPs. Bill Gates sugarcoated the Mac and Steve Jobs loved every moment of it.

Steve Jobs and Bill Gates were so close at the time that according to a Guardian source, they even double-dated occasionally.

But all good things must end.

Rivals (1983 to 1996)

Steve Jobs had this dream where Apple would dominate the computer business and Microsoft would own the application-side of that business. The OS would naturally also by controlled by Apple.

But Bill Gates wasn't blind. He understood that the Graphical User Interface was the future of computing. He also knew that it would quickly make its DOS operating system irrelevant and threatens Microsoft to become (just) a software company dependent of Apple. Bill Gates had bigger plans.

For years, Microsoft had engineers secretly copying the Macintosh OS and working on its own version of a Graphical OS: Windows. Not long after the Internal Event in Hawaii, Steve Jobs learned the crushing news. Microsoft wanted to compete with Apple; Bill Gates deceived him.

For the next 15 years, Apple would engage in a strange relationship with Microsoft. On one end, Microsoft was prying marketshare away from Apple, on the other, it was one of its biggest partner. Steve Jobs would soon leave Apple and create NeXT but would not succeed to make a dent in Microsoft's dominance.

Along the way, Jobs often sparred with Microsoft, criticizing the company's lack of creativity.

"The only problem with Microsoft is they just have no taste," Jobs said in the 1996 public television documentary "Triumph of the Nerds." "They have absolutely no taste. And I don't mean that in a small way, I mean that in a big way, in the sense that they don't think of original ideas, and they don't bring much culture into their products."

In a New York Times article that ran after the documentary aired, Jobs disclosed that he called Gates afterward to apologize. But only to a degree.

"I told him I believed every word of what I'd said but that I never should have said it in public," Jobs told the Times. "I wish him the best, I really do. I just think he and Microsoft are a bit narrow. He'd be a broader guy if he had dropped acid once or gone off to an ashram when he was younger."

Truce (1997 to 2002)

Things changed when Steve Jobs came back at Apple in 1997. On the brink of bankruptcy, Jobs turned to his 'old acquaintance' Bill Gates for help.

The Microsoft Deal is considered a low point in Apple's history by many.

When Steve Jobs announced that Microsoft was not the enemy anymore, few could believe their ears. He went as far as praising the quality of their Mac apps like Office and Internet Explorer… that was outrageous!

Things were weird for a few years – 5 years to be exact. Which corresponds to the 5 years of the 'Microsoft Deal'. During that period Steve Jobs only had good things to say about Redmond. But it was an illusion. If Bill Gates was a great liar, Steve Jobs was his equal.

Frenemies (2003 to 2011)

It's now 2003 and iPods are selling like hotcakes. The Apple brand is cool again.

Apple understood it could not compete with Microsoft on the desktop so it brought the battle to another field: mobile. Here, Microsoft is a minor player. Apple doesn't need Microsoft like it did at the turn of the millenium. So Steve doesn't have to play nice anymore.

Apple's tone of voice about Redmond suddenly changes.

The Get Mac campaign hits the airwaves and pokes fun of the PC industry and Microsoft (watch this All Things D interview with Steve Jobs and Bill Gates were Bill is compared to the PC guy!).

The praising days are over.

Was Steve Jobs still bitter at Bill Gates and Microsoft after all these years?

Steve's sudden change of attitude towards Microsoft in the mid-00s seems to indicate that.

There's however an event that is even more striking. During All Things D5 in 2007, Steve Jobs and Bill Gates were 'finally' reunited on a stage. Steve was given the opportunity to praise Bill Gates when asked what Bill's contribution to the PC industry was. Steve's answer was rather generic: "Bill was the first to truly see the value of software." That's all.

But if Steve was still bitter about Bill, why would he keep a letter of Bill next to his bed during his last moments?

Though to say...

What both men really thought of each others or what really happened behind the curtain will probably never be known. You have to hope that these titans truly shared mutual respects and eventually found grounds to appreciate each others.

Bill Gates statement at the passing of Steve Jobs

I'm truly saddened to learn of Steve Jobs' death. Melinda and I extend our sincere condolences to his family and friends, and to everyone Steve has touched through his work.

Steve and I first met nearly 30 years ago, and have been colleagues, competitors, and friends over the course of more than half our lives.

The world rarely sees someone who has had the profound impact Steve has had, the effects of which will be felt for many generations to come.

For those of us lucky enough to get to work with him, it's been an insanely great honor. I will miss Steve immensely.

THINGS YOU DON'T KNOW ABOUT BILL GATES

What are the first three things that come to your mind when you hear the name 'Bill Gates'?

1. He's the richest man in the world with a net worth of $79 billion.

2. He is the co-founder of Microsoft, the world's largest and most successful PC software company.

3. He is the world's most prolific humanitarian who donates generously through the Bill & Melinda Gates Foundation.

Besides his philanthropic efforts and online presence, there are lot of things about Gates that you probably didn't know. While there are many unknown facts about Gates, we bring to you the top 15 surprising facts about him:

1. Born as William Henry Gates III, Bill's nickname as a child was "Trey," reflective of The Third" following his moniker, as he was the fourth consecutive Gates man of the same name.

2. Gates wrote his first computer program on a General Electric computer as a young teenager at Lakeside Prep School. It was a version of tic-tac-toe, where you could play against the computer.

3. Once his school discovered Gates' coding abilities, they let him write the school's computer program for scheduling students in classes. Apparently, he slyly altered the code so that he would get placed in classes with mostly female students.

4. Gates scored 1590 out of 1600 on his SATs.

5. Gates, Paul Allen and Paul Gilbert launched a company while Gates and Allen were still students at Lakeside School in Seattle. Their Traf-O-Data 8008 computer was designed to read data from roadside traffic counters and create reports for traffic engineers.

6. Gates was a college dropout. He left Harvard University in 1975 to fully devote himself to Microsoft.

7. Gates was arrested in New Mexico in 1977, for jumping a red-light and driving without a licence.

8. Bill Gates aimed to become a millionaire by the age of 30. However, he became a billionaire at 31.

9. At Microsoft, Gates used to memorize employees' license plates to keep tabs on their comings and goings. "Eventually I had to loosen up, as the company got to a reasonable size," he said.

10. In 1994, he was asked by a TV interviewer if he could jump over a chair

from a standing position. Gates promptly took the challenge and leaped over the chair like a boss.

11. One of Gates' biggest splurges was the Codex Leicester, a collection of writings by Leonardo da Vinci. He acquired it at 1994 auction for $30.8 million.

12. He flew coach until 1997, even though his net worth was already well into the double-digit billions.

13. Despite his immense wealth, Gates doesn't believe in leaving children a ton of money as inheritance; his three kids (daughters Jennifer and Phoebe and son Rory) will inherit only $10 million each — just a fraction of his $81.1 billion net worth. "Leaving kids massive amounts of money is not a favor to them," he says.

Conclusion

Bill Gates career has been marked by his incredible vision. Microsoft beat out the competition largely because they were always looking one step ahead, to the next revolutionary idea.

The lesson here: if you want to get ahead in business, think ahead.

Gates was still thinking ahead when he retired from Microsoft in 2008. He told PC Mag that he thought the Tablet PCs, Internet TV, and natural user interface would be thriving in the near future. History is proving him right.

So, if Gates knew what was coming next, why didn't he stick around to make it happen? Surely, he could have added a few billion more to his bank accounts.

The answer is that, at some point while thinking about the future, Gates started giving more importance to health care, poverty, and education than he did to the next hi-tech gizmo. He's making a bigger impact on the future through The Bill &

Melinda Gates Foundation than he would have made by continuing to run Microsoft.

Bill Gates was a multi-faceted leader. He had no problem communicating how he wanted things done, or in getting those things done. However, he was not the best at listening to others ideas. He was not one to compromise on his own ideas either. Gates was a charismatic leader who fits well under the path-goal theory by Robbins and Judge (2014). Gates used his position as CEO at Microsoft to not only influence his employees, but also those he worked with or came in contact with. Gates was not very politically minded, he focused more on power and profit. Although this may have created some conflicts in his career, Gates thrived on conflict. Just as Gates was always looking for problems to solve, he was creating conflict to motivate his employees to find better outcomes.

In order to deliver in business and life, a person needs to learn how to survive the tough times, take a visionary position, use the opportunity coming along the way and work on merit –all the time. Lastly, it's not always the genius or hard work which counts. Along with hard work, being at the right place at the right time is equally important!

Ultimately, Bill Gates is one of the greatest modern-day leaders. He pioneered the technology revolution and put the layer between the user and DOS. He made a living room-sized computer into a coffee table sized computer. Bill Gates has become the richest person in the world and donated most of his money. He has also founded the Bill & Melinda Gates Foundation to help fight multiple causes. He continues to live his life making a difference in this world.